Digital Learning Series
A Series by Post-Technology Educators

To the extent that education is the engagement of individual learners to knowledge, the Internet has changed everything because knowledge has moved to a new location. What is known by humankind is now located primarily on the Internet, and what is not there today will be soon.

The great migration of knowledge into cyberspace has kicked off a technological revolution in education. Teachers have marched off to computer classes. Librarians have been retrotrained as technology specialists. The "crayon set" can type before they're in kindergarten, and coding is a second language for the generation of kids now in high school. Millions of dollars have been spent wiring schools, and millions more are being spent reworking the wiring to broadcast the Internet to mobile receivers.

All the technological advances, both in equipment and user skills, have certainly been crucial to engaging knowledge on the Internet. But there is a further necessary component to the new education era introduced by the Internet. This book series swings the focus from the technology of connectivity to the digital form and substance of the knowledge engaged by learners on the Internet. Where is the information and how do we find it? In what form does it appear? How do we learn it? How do we teach it? These are real questions encountered every day in classroom teaching, independent study, and the preparation of online learning materials.

We can answer these questions by realizing that the interesting challenges today are no longer technical. True innovation is concerned with creating learning resources in the digital milieu. It is technically possible to link to almost anything on the Internet, but how do we choose what to link to in order to create an effective learning environment? Teaching and learning knowledge in its new location require tools that are *cognitively* new, though no longer *technically* so. How does interactive multimedia connected to a stunningly rich context web make learning grammar or geography or genetics different from studying these subjects in an isolated classroom or book? How can I implement the advantages and minimize the disadvantages in my own teaching and learning? These and many other such immediate and important questions arise once we become competent on the technical side.

The authors who have written books for this series are active participants in the challenges of engaging individual learners to the Internet, describing the reconnection to knowledge in our post-technology education world.

Judy Breck, Series Editor
New York City
September 2003

Digital Learning Series
Edited by Judy Breck

Teaching and Learning with Technology

Learning Where to Look

Noah Kravitz

Digital Learning, No. 2

ScarecrowEducation
Lanham, Maryland • Toronto • Oxford
2004

Published in the United States of America
by ScarecrowEducation
An imprint of The Rowman & Littlefield Publishing Group, Inc.
4501 Forbes Boulevard, Suite 200, Lanham, Maryland 20706
www.scneroweducation.com

PO Box 317
Oxford
OX2 9RU, UK

British Library Cataloguing in Publication Information Available

Library of Congress Cataloging-in-Publication Data

Kravitz, Noah, 1973–
    Teaching and learning with technology : learning where to look / Noah
  Kravitz.
        p. cm. — (Digital learning ; no. 2)
    Includes bibliographical references and index.
    ISBN 1-57886-117-9 (pbk. : alk. paper)
    1. Educational technology. 2. Internet in education. I. Title. II. Series.
LB1028.3.K73 2004
371.33'4–dc22   2003026497

For all of the teachers and students who have taught me and for those from whom I hope to learn for a long time to come.

Contents

Acknowledgments

I would first like to thank Judy Breck for presenting me with the opportunity to write this book. Although I had written extensively on the subject in shorter formats, the idea of writing a full-length book on educational technology honestly hadn't crossed my mind until Judy approached me about it. For the opportunity, inspiration, and guidance along the way—let alone the faith in me to meet the challenge—I thank Judy from the bottom of my heart.

Also, to Tom Koerner and Cindy Tursman at ScarecrowEducation a big thank-you for deciding to actually publish what I've written, and a special thanks to Sally Craley, my editor, whose perspective, patience, and understanding of the ways real life can meddle with a production schedule have been greatly appreciated.

This book literally could not have been written without the influence of all of the people I've learned with and from throughout my life. In particular I'd like to thank Dr. Nedra Stimpfle and Mrs. Irene Jovell of Niskayuna High School who taught me a lot about English, math, and life during one of the hardest times in my growing up. Also, Jane Condliffe, Lynette Guastaferro, and Alvarez Symonette at Teaching Matters, Dr. Marvin Cohen and Hal Melnick at the Bank Street College of Education, Katie McMillan Culp and her cohorts at the Center for Children and Technology, Grace Meo and the rest of the Center for Applied Special Technology (CAST) in Wakefield, Massachusetts, and Laura Koller at MIT (formerly of MIT OpenCourseWare) all proved invaluable resources in my researching, writing, and editing, be they people I interviewed, called upon to read early drafts, or simply had the chance to work with on various projects.

Amy Hundley at Grove/Atlantic, Jessica Holahan at Sanford Green-berger, and Jennifer Farthing at Kaplan all assisted me with their invaluable (and free) advice on the publishing world, and to them I owe a great deal of gratitude.

Margaret, my partner in crime, teaching, and life, not only lent her expertise on education and publishing, but also decided somewhere in the middle of my writing this book to share a home with me, and thus signed on to give me even more of her love, support, insight, and editing services than she already had been. This—let alone the rest of my life—would be so much less without you than it is now. Thank you.

And to my parents, who have taught me the most of all, I say thanks for your love, support, and ongoing understanding of who I am and hope to be. Your understanding of what really matters in this world has become a part of me, and I only hope to pass that on to others.

Introduction

One of the main reasons I work with technology is there is literally always something new to learn. The pervasiveness of computerized technology in nearly all facets of 21st-century life combined with the incredible rate of progress in the fields of computing and telecommunications mean that there will always be something for me to learn—far more than I could ever hope to learn, actually.

Another reason I enjoy technology, I've come to realize, is I enjoy teaching people how to use it. Whether it's helping my mom and dad hook up their new laptop to the wireless Internet connection at their house or teaching a class of nine-year-olds how to type, I really enjoy the process of sharing knowledge with others and then watching how they make it their own. Any frustrations inherent in teaching—and believe me, I get frustrated sometimes—are well worth the joy that is returned to me in seeing a student step through that door into a brand-new part of the world. Furthermore, *I* always learn something—be it about myself, my student, or the subject matter—in the process.

Once I dug into the thinking, researching, and writing of *Teaching and Learning with Technology: Learning Where to Look*, I quickly realized that my challenge would not be finding things to say about educational technology but rather deciding what to leave out. Much has changed and advanced in the fields of education and technology even in the course of my writing; my fears quickly evolved from doubting I could write the book to wondering if it would be outdated before I'd even gotten it onto the publisher's desk. Thankfully, text travels pretty quickly over e-mail.

If you take nothing else from reading this book, I hope you come away with the central message of the six chapters that follow: Education is about trying to better understand ourselves, our world, and the people we share it with, and technology is a very powerful tool that can be used to help us attain that understanding. Technology is not a magic elixir for what ails us, nor is it a replacement for teachers, role models, or any other people in our lives. Technology, and any computing device connected to the Internet in particular, is a versatile tool that can help us gather, process, and share information to great ends. The varying methods with which a personal computer allows us to express information, and the speed and power with which we can process and transmit that information, are growing by leaps and bounds every day. What we have seen now, at the beginning of the 21st century, in the way of the potential of networked computing is literally just the tip of the iceberg. Amazing times await us, to be certain.

But whatever the future may bring in the way of electronic fibers in our clothing that can change colors with the click of a button, hydrogen-powered hovercrafts taking the kids to soccer practice, and nanobots that treat and prevent disease from within the cells of our bodies themselves, the technology is nothing without our humanity to guide it. By the end of this century, technology will play more of a role in the functioning of our world than we could possibly imagine. It will be up to us to decide how to harness this science for the betterment of us all.

Of course, I'm sure more than one pundit said something similar back around 1903, as well. . . .

Chapter one is a brief history of the print revolution. Understanding how print—specifically, the invention of the Gutenberg movable-type printing press—gave birth to the age of mass communication is crucial to being able to think about the role that the personal computer, digital media, and Internet will have in the information revolution that will define the 21st century. Much as the ability to print, reproduce, and disseminate thoughts, ideas, and information led to cultural and political change in 16th-century Europe, so do the broadcast and organizational powers of the Internet promise to reorganize our world of nation-states into a true global community in the years to come.

Chapter two is a beginning look at educational technology, and a hands-on overview of how to think about using computers and the Internet in teaching situations. From the basics of manning the keyboard and mouse and managing files, to thinking about filtering software and online safety, preparing yourself to use technology in your teaching is the best way to ensure that your students get the most out of instructional time. Personal computers are powerful allies for your students to have in whatever they're studying, both now and in the future, so it is important that you help them to become computer literate. Just as my high school guidance counselor implored me to learn to type (and for once, I listened to him), I say to you: "Teach your students to surf!" As information becomes more plentiful and accessible in the next ten to twenty years, knowing how to find information efficiently and effectively will become one of the most valuable skills your students possess.

Chapter three moves further into the specifics of using the Internet for teaching and learning. From search-engine strategies to a look at HTML to some of the other technologies that make the web work, this chapter gets inside the technology itself from an educator's point of view. Where are the best places to look online for educational resources? Are there any good sites out there for teaching third graders about fossils? What's a WYSIWYG and a PIM? And what does an Internet-ready kitchen have to do with the future of education? The answers to these and many other questions are yours for the finding in chapter three.

Chapter four centers on *ubiquitous tools*, a term I learned from Dr. Marvin Cohen of the Bank Street College for Education. Ubiquitous tools are the tools of everyday life that we are all familiar with. When it comes to technology, this means e-mail, web surfing, word processing, and PowerPoint. Rather than spending lots of time and money on scores of specifically targeted educational software, how can we make use of these ubiquitous tools to help teach reading and writing, math, and social studies? Using ubiquitous tools in our classrooms not only frees up resources we might otherwise spend acquiring and learning customized software but it also serves the secondary purpose of reinforcing student mastery of these tools that are fast becoming part and parcel of life in the modern world. This chapter contains some of the philosophy behind the theory of ubiquitous tools as well as real-world examples of the tools in action.

Chapter five looks at literacy in the information age. Literacy has long been at the core of educational triumphs and failures; we're constantly hearing about literacy rates and the problems of illiteracy that our nation faces. We have traditionally thought of literacy in terms of reading and writing, but the truth is that more and more often we are expected to make sense of myriad forms of information that are thrust upon us from the moment we wake up in the morning until we go to sleep at night. Television, radio, movies, advertisements, newspapers, and magazines—information comes at us in text and imagery, still and moving, in print, and through sound. With the advent of computers and the Internet in the classroom and beyond, teachers and students must learn to access all forms of digital media. Nowadays it is easier than ever to both access and produce words, images, audio, and video, and even interactive media, and it will only get easier with time. How can we teach our students to decode a photograph and use it as a historical document? Is this a valuable skill for them to learn? How can we ourselves learn to understand and value a student's multimedia presentation as a response to an assignment? Or should we even accept multimedia as a worthy form of expression when so many in our world still struggle to read and write? These are all part of the debate over literacy that will grow as more and more computers find their way into our schools and classrooms.

Finally, chapter six is a conclusion: some thoughts on where we've come from and some hopes and questions for the future. Technology certainly isn't going away, so how can we think about how to best harness it for our future and our children's future?

As human beings, we are constantly learning from and about one another. As educators we have chosen to make a life out of studying and improving the processes by which we teach and learn. In writing this book I hope to share some of my thoughts and ideas on how you can use technology to aid you in your work, and my greatest wish is that you can take something from my thoughts with you, improve upon it, and teach it to someone else so they might make it even better for generations to come.

Chapter One

The Revolution Is Being Webcast

JOHANNES GUTENBERG AND THE PRINT REVOLUTION

Half a millennium ago, Johannes Gutenberg invented the movable-type printing press. Gutenberg, a German goldsmith living in the mid-15th century, didn't set out to revolutionize modern communications. Rather, he followed the age-old practice of savvy businessmen in any field: he identified a need and tried to fill it. Times were changing in Europe and both the Church and secular employers were hiring all of the literate scribes they could find to copy and disseminate texts. In the two hundred or so years since rag paper had made its European debut, production techniques had been refined to make the medium cheap and plentiful throughout the land, but texts still had to be written out by hand.[1]

There were no typewriters, mimeograph machines, or printing presses. Between indulgences and sacred texts being printed by the Church and secular documents pertaining in large part to expanding governments and newly burgeoning trade systems, the demand for text reproduction simply couldn't be met by scribes working manually. Gutenberg saw this and knew that an affordable and efficient printing press capable of mass-producing different documents would make a killing. So he combined elements of some existing technologies with his own bit of genius — a very clever system of molding and casting movable metal type — and the Gutenberg printing press was born.

Of course, no press is worth a dime without text to reproduce, so Gutenberg designed his own Latin version of the most popular book ever, and ran off three hundred copies of the Gutenberg Bible. Perhaps

Johannes was a better inventor than businessman (or else he committed some hubris in christening his invention with a bible named for himself): the inventor of one of the foremost technologies of modern times somehow ran himself into bankruptcy not long after his invention caught on. Still, the movable-type press stuck around and is often credited as one of the driving forces behind the cultural and intellectual revolution that swept through Europe in the years following its invention.[2]

The impact of Gutenberg's press and the print revolution that followed is inestimable. Before the printing press, texts were rarified objects, handwritten and hard to come by, objects of status as much as of function. When the commoner was made privy to a text, it was almost always through his listening to a public reading, not by reading the document himself. In fact, most citizens of the day were illiterate.

The notion of reading that we now take for granted, an individual silently scanning and interpreting a text just as you are probably doing now, was anything but commonplace before the Gutenberg press. All of the things that we now do with a text—taking the newspaper with us when we leave home, rereading a book and making notes in the margin, even passing a favorite story or article along to a friend or colleague—were all but impossible before Gutenberg. Before the press, the only books that existed were handwritten, and those were difficult to come by if you weren't a man of the cloth or had some similar stature.

Along with the newfound access to literacy that the movable press afforded came an unprecedented ability to document and share information. Imagine trying to bake a cake, assemble a bicycle, or operate a computer for the first time without directions to guide you through the process. You could try, but without some prior experience you wouldn't really know where to begin. Now imagine trying to conduct more involved scientific inquiries or mathematical undertakings without the documented research of your contemporaries or those who came before you. The invention and widespread adoption of Gutenberg's printing press dramatically expanded intellectual exploration and collaboration, and was vital to the spread of revolutionary cultural and social thought. Never before had people been able to share their discoveries and opinions with such large audiences without considerable travel to meet them in person. Thanks to Gutenberg, a person with an idea could, for the first time, widely disseminate that idea via the written word.

The effects of the print revolution on European society in the 15th century and beyond have been widely documented to include the Reformation, a newfound emphasis on the rights and private lives of individuals, and the birth of formalized scientific inquiry and procedures. The mere object you hold before you now is evidence that a great idea can change the world.

"ALL THE NEWS OF THE DAY"

A little less than two hundred years after the movable-type press swept through Europe, the first machine of its kind made its way to the shores of America—then the American colonies—in 1638. Stephen Daye of Cambridge, Massachusetts, brought a press over and he and his son Matthew began to experiment with it. Two years later, 1,700 copies of the *Bay Psalm Book* were printed and the colonies had their first mass-printed text.

The same spirit of personal and intellectual freedom that brought about change in Europe in Gutenberg's time caught fire in the colonies in the days leading up to 1776. When, soon after, the paper roll was developed in the early 1800s, that spirit of freedom was spread via newsprint throughout the land. Rolled-up paper may not seem like such a technological breakthrough by itself, but combined with changes to the mechanical press it spurred on major advancements in the efficiency of large-scale printing operations. The paper roll, in fact, allowed Benjamin Day to drop the price of his newspaper, *New York Sun*, to one penny per copy in 1833. As Day himself said, the *Sun* was meant "to lay before the public, at a price well within the means of everyone, all the news of the day."

The penny press, as Day's newspaper machine is now called, is arguably the true beginning of mass media. The invention and refinement of the printing press changed the way the Western world communicated. As a result, individuals had the chance to be heard by the masses. Intellectuals found contemporaries and developed schools of thought that changed the way people viewed and governed themselves. Citizens found means to organize themselves on a wide scale and broke free from religious and political oppression. And the ability to read and write took on the utmost importance among once illiterate peoples.

What is happening now, at the beginning of the 21st century, is in many ways similar to what happened in the years following Johannes Gutenberg's invention of the printing press. We are in the midst of an intellectual and societal revolution, one that is already changing many of us in profound ways and will continue to do so for generations to come. The advent of the personal computer and the Internet that followed it has begun a sea change that is making mass communication both more efficient than ever and also giving rise to an interactive medium the likes of which we've never before seen.

Although the nature of communication has always, by definition, been interactive, modern telecommunications allow for receivers of information to also act as broadcasters capable of reaching multiple audiences with a single transmission. Just think of the difference between a handwritten letter sent to one addressee through the postal service and an electronic message e-mailed to many recipients all at once. The ease with which we communicate with groups of people (and the ease with which they, in turn, can amend, forward, and respond to those communications to reach even more people) has increased tenfold since the Internet took hold of the Western world. That level of ease only promises to grow in the coming years.

Though it may be possible to point to a handful of ideas like Gutenberg's press that set the wave of mass communications in motion, this revolution is not so easily captured in one all-encompassing word such as "print." This revolution is about many mediums and the abilities of many people to use and combine them in ways we're only just beginning to see and imagine. From broadcast radio and television to interactive, digital versions of each streamed across the web, communication technology advanced by leaps and bounds during the 1900s and is only gaining steam as we begin the 21st century.

This book is about the technology of communication, the revolution people are creating and experiencing with that technology, and its specific impact on the ways in which we teach and learn from one another. Though we in the Western world have begun to see the effects of the revolution in the past decade through the transmission of text, images, and sound over the Internet, it would not suffice to call this the Internet revolution. The Internet is really just the name for the network of connected computers and gadgets that we're building across the globe. What's important isn't just the network, but what we do with it: what information we choose to share over the network and how we reinvent the network itself to accommodate and expand the types of information we can share.

Gutenberg's press was nothing without the print that came off of it; our Internet is nothing without the information we share across it. The revolution we are part of now encompasses all forms of information—audio, visual, textual, and combinations thereof—and so we can call our revolution the "information revolution."

THE INFORMATION REVOLUTION

My senior year of college spanned 1994–1995. During that time I worked in the café of the campus bookstore in a small town in Connecticut. There weren't too many places to go in town for a decent cup of coffee, and the bookstore café had the added advantage of letting students charge textbooks and food to their student accounts, a.k.a. "The bill Mom and Dad get." So the café was a popular place among the student body.

One guy, a senior named Paul, would come into the café every so often during the afternoon, order a cup of black coffee, and sit down at a table by himself. He usually carried a mysterious magazine within a padded manila envelope. One slow afternoon while the boss was away, Paul let me in on his secret reading habit.

"It's called *Wired*," he explained. "My mom gets them from the newsstand back home in Oregon and sends them to me. Can't get 'em on the East Coast yet."

"What is it?" I asked.

"The future," he smiled. "Technology stuff, mostly about the web. I'm teaching myself HTML."

Paul must have seen the perplexed look on my face, because he went on.

"Home pages," he said. "HTML's the code you use to write home pages." Code meant programming, this I knew. But what in the world was a home page?

"The web's the future," Paul continued. "In a few years, companies are going to be paying people thousands of dollars to make home pages for them. Everyone's going to want a website. Big money, and it's pretty easy."

"Huh," I said, walking back to the counter. A fifty-cent tip from another customer awaited me.

Paul was almost right—not a decade later the World Wide Web had become big business in America and he was running his own online travel service from offices in Vermont. But companies weren't just paying thousands of dollars for their websites to be built. The documentary film *Startup.Com*, released in 2001, chronicles the rise and fall of one fledgling online business (govworks.com) that shelled out just short of $10 million for a very complex website that, upon launch, didn't even work. This is just one of countless stories that chronicle the excesses of the "dot-com" years.

The Internet as we know it grew out of a Pentagon-contracted project designed to let government researchers share their findings more efficiently and effectively. ARPANET was brought online in 1969 and went international in 1973. In 1990 ARPANET was brought down, and a year later a new protocol for online communications was adopted as the worldwide standard of choice. This protocol, invented by Tim Berners-Lee at CERN, the European Laboratory for Particle Physics, was called WWW—short for World Wide Web.

My first interaction with the Net was during college when I spent many a night in front of the old VAX terminals in the computer lab sending e-mails to my faraway then-girlfriend. We were in love, at different schools some eight hours away by car, and too broke to talk on the phone very much, so we learned how to use e-mail. Then we learned to instantly message each other using a basic UNIX line command, so we'd make "chat dates," whiling the hours away typing to each other in real time. I think we were limited to one line of text at a time this way, and she was nestled in her cozy dorm room while I sat under the cold fluorescent lights of the science center, but who ever said love was easy?

Then came sophomore year when I discovered the joys of online bulletin boards. Still on the VAX—picture the gray plastic computers of the '80s that housed giant monochrome CRT monitors with phone cord-tethered keyboards coming out of them—I scanned page after page of text-only message boards, alphabetized by subjects ranging from abstract art to zoology. People all over the world were using the boards to discuss topics of personal and professional interest, argue about politics and sports teams, and forge online friendships with electronic pen pals they'd never seen in person.

Just to put things in perspective, "modern" 56K dial-up modems that are soon to go the way of the dinosaurs can receive data at 56.6 thousand bits per second, or about 25 times as fast as those modems that the first "Netizens" (Internet citizens) were using to brave cyberspace with. DSL and cable modems now being installed in more and more homes, and the T1 and T3 lines that many businesses and universities use, move data at rates up to and beyond 1,500,000 bits per second (1.5 Mbps), which is thirty or more times the speed of a 56K modem and light years faster than those first 2,400-baud units. The speed and volume at which data travels is often referred to as bandwidth. Combined with advances in compression technology (packing more useful information into a smaller chunk of data), increased bandwidth has turned those first residential streets of Net access into today's vaunted "information superhighway." Traffic online will only get faster—and denser—as time goes on.

When I was in elementary school, my family was fortunate to have a TRS-80 computer at home. Yes, the same TRS-80 that you could buy at RadioShack in the mall. Then my elementary school got an Apple II and soon enough we had one of those, too, replete with a monochrome green screen and state-of-the-art floppy disc drive. (The TRS-80 had a tape drive, so this was hi-tech!) The high school paper I mentioned was published entirely on Apple Macintoshes running Aldus Pagemaker software. I went to a good public school, but it was still a school and not corporate America, which had embraced desktop publishing in full force a few years prior at the end of the 1980s, and was running fancier computers by this time.

So first it was the word processor, then desktop publishing, and then in the mid-1990s the Internet struck. And struck it did. My own career path, to some humble extent, has so far paralleled the trajectory of the Net's impact on the Western world. From that first job publishing newsletters for Barnard College, I went to a small consulting company in New York where I did everything from editing promotional videos using a souped-up Mac to troubleshooting computer networks for ad agencies. This wasn't even a decade ago, but video editing was pricey stuff then; nowadays, all new PCs come equipped ready to turn your home movie footage into polished silver screen features, but way back in 1996 you needed special digitizing boards and ultrafast hard drives that ran your costs into the tens of thousands of dollars. So getting the chance to play around with this stuff at work was a big, nerdy thrill for me.

Though I first remember seeing a proper web page on a personal computer (in the Mac lab that opened just beyond the room full of VAXes) during my senior year at school, it wasn't until after graduation when I had my first office job that I began to understand what was really going on behind those three W's that people were starting to talk a lot about. Having moved to New York to pursue a career in journalism, I landed a part-time job doing desktop publishing with skills I'd honed in my two years as sports editor of my high school paper. The Macintosh computer on my desk in New York was bigger and faster than the Mac Classics we'd had in high school, but the publishing software was basically the same. The job was pretty easy, and once I had my biweekly newsletter proofed, printed, and sent to the copy room, I generally found myself with free time before I had to set about folding and mailing them out to subscribers.

This is when I discovered the World Wide Web.

FROM MOVABLE TEXT TO HYPERTEXT

During the years leading up to the Gutenberg press, the publishing industry in Europe was approaching a critical mass. "Scribal monks sanctioned by the Church had overseen the maintenance and hand-copying of scripts for centuries, but the secular world began to foster its own version of the scribal copyist profession. The many new scriptoria, or writing shops, that sprang up employed virtually every literate cleric who wanted work."[3]

Scan forward five centuries and you'll find me, the "literate cleric" who wanted work and found it copying and setting text for distribution. Granted, I was using a keyboard and mouse to cut and paste instead of pen and ink to hand copy, but the idea was the same: literate workers were needed to meet the increasing demand for mass-produced published materials.

I trace my own career path here to provide a tangible line with which to draw parallels between the historical moment that happened beginning in the 1450s with the Gutenberg press and the one that began with the widespread commercial and cultural adoption of the Internet in the West in the mid-1990s. Just as the *scriptoria* of Gutenberg's day would soon give way to the automated world of the print house and its movable-type press, so too was our late 20th-century world of desktop publishing and photocopying about to begin the inevitable process of ceding to a newer, better technology: networked computing and HyperText Markup Language (HTML).

The greatest thing about HTML is that it's inherently easy to access, copy, and co-opt. In other words, it was built to be learned from. When I first stumbled across web pages from my desk in Manhattan in 1995, I wanted to know how they worked. Fortunately, my web browser featured a nifty command called "View Source" that was meant to tell me just that. View Source would take a nicely formatted web page full of stylized text, meticulously designed art, and programmed hyperlinks and break it down into its nuts and bolts—the HTML code behind the scenes.

The best part was that good programmers are trained to tag their code with comments, which are like author's notes that explain a complicated text to readers who come along later to decipher it. Comments in a computer program's source code break the code apart into logical chunks. An HTML page, for instance, might have comments that read <!—Begin Top Ad Frame—> and <!—Begin Body Text—>. These comments don't add anything to the functionality of the program itself, but rather act like chapter headings for the program, designating the parts of the code that will render an advertisement at the top of a page and the main body of text in the page, respectively. So not only did I get to see the source code for almost any web page I wanted, I often could learn from the notes that master coders left behind for me.

From the beginning, the web was about sharing. Words like community and collaborative get thrown around a lot these days in marketing conferences, but they also hold weight when it comes to what people actually do online. Chat rooms, bulletin boards, instant messaging—all of this is immensely popular, and all of it is about communicating with other people. Programmers, like most scientists I've encountered, tend to be an interesting breed, often intensely self-contained yet incredibly willing to share their knowledge. For programmers, it's all about learning to do a task as efficiently and elegantly as possible. There's no better way to learn a new trick than by watching someone else do it and then trying for yourself. So not long after HTML caught on and web pages started popping up all over the Net, web pages *about* making web pages started to pop up, too.

As you probably know, the five years between 1996 an[d] wild time for the American and global economy. The dot-c[om] hold of the United States and didn't let go until the bubble had to burst. Again, thinking back to Gutenberg's time, all clerics who wanted work had it—it's just that they were o[n] a changing definition of what constituted *literacy*. Where 1[5th-] century Europe spawned *print literacy*, late 20th-century Am[erica] a new term: *computer literacy*.

Computer literacy might best be thought of as an importa[nt] of the larger subset known as *media literacy*. Media critics McLuhan, Fredric Jameson, and Walter Benjamin spent the m[ost of] the 20th century racking their brains and lecturing their dis[ciples] artistic, cultural, and economic impacts that newly develope[d] newspapers, magazines, radio, film, and television—were ha[ving on soci-] ety.[4] The computer itself may have been born more out of scie[nce] than cultural needs, but the shrinking microchip gave way in [the lat-] ter of the century to computers that fit on a desk instead of tak[ing an en-] tire room. Though the price was initially quite high, people st[arted buying] home computers, and new companies popped up to meet the d[emand and] then outdo each other in the areas of personal computer hardw[are and soft-] ware development.

During the middle part of the 1980s, desktop publishing [was the] first compelling reason for mainstream America to want to [a com-] puter. From simple word processing to more advanced page [layout and] graphic design, PCs and home printers were becoming affor[dable and] sophisticated—enough to bump the old typewriter off its s[pot on the] desk in the den. The ability to edit text without printing, cu[t and paste] words instead of retyping them by hand, and augment your [writing] with fancy formatting and artwork took do-it-yourselfers by s[torm. From] neighborhood newsletters to corporate publications, the abil[ity to read] and write was now complemented by the ability to edit, fo[rmat, and] print.

Additionally, the more hardcore hobbyists among PC owners [were] chasing 2,400-and 9,600-baud modems and logging on to text-[based bul-] letin board systems (BBS). These BBS were the public offsh[oot of the] military's ARPANET network and really were the precursor t[o what we] now think of as the Internet.

TELEPHONES, CHAT ROOMS, AND CONVERGENCE

Soon enough, though, I left that job to pursue a graduate degree in education. During my first summer session at grad school I happened upon an ad in search of computer teachers for a private school in Brooklyn and the rest is history in the making. I taught by day and learned by night, and often vice versa. For as advanced as I thought I was in the use of computers for creating everything from newsletters to documentary movies, the kids I was working with showed me something I'd never really thought about before, something that was and is destined to be the future of the Net.

Since their invention in 1876, telephones have been the bane of existence for many a teenager and many more a teenager's parents. What adult who grew up in the past fifty or so years—especially those who've had teenage children of their own—can't remember a night when the family telephone was monopolized by gossiping about who did what in class that day or who was seen with whom after school? People tell stories to make sense of the things that happen in their lives and teenagers are no different—except maybe that they like to do it a little more than the rest of us.

The junior high school students I taught came largely from upper-middle-class backgrounds and they lived in New York City, so they may have been a little ahead of the curve when it came to the level of privilege and sophistication in their home lives. Then again, maybe the average American teenager at the turn of the millennium spent hours a night gossiping in chat rooms. These kids certainly did.

At the time, I was taking a graduate class in theories of communication that included a substantial online component. Students were expected to participate in an asynchronous forum in which we posted our thoughts on various topics and held forth in debates with one another via an Internet message board set up specifically for our class. I really enjoyed the class and the online discussions, so I logged on a lot while doing my class work after teaching. One day I mentioned the class to some of my eighth graders and asked them if they spent time online at home. I wasn't surprised to find out that they did, but what amazed me was the amount of time they claimed to spend each night just hanging out in chat rooms—talking and gossiping about the day's events online much as I did on the telephone as a thirteen-year-old.

Most of the students who hung out in chat rooms did so in conjunction with surfing the web, watching TV, and even doing homework and talking on the telephone. Holding forth in multiple conversations via chat room, instant messenger, and the telephone was not uncommon, and circulation of "surveys" ("Who's the cutest freshman?" "Which teacher has the worst breath?" and so forth) via mass e-mail was also popular.

Another remarkable behavior was the speed with which these kids found and directed each other to items of interest online. URLs to websites about their favorite pop singers, sports teams, and movie stars were passed around with aplomb. Links to research sites for homework—and reviews of the newest video games—were traded as quickly as they were found. Teens today know what a tremendous resource the Net is because they've been raised on it. Much as I was shown the basics of how to use the card catalogue in the public library and soon found myself pulling from the shelves books on all the topics I could think of, so too has this generation been shown the basics of using a search engine and downloading files. Now they find what they need online and take it in digital form to use on their computers.

In the fifteen or so years since those first Netizens started populating text-only BBS via painfully slow 2,400-baud modems, the phenomenon of online communication in America had swelled to the point of junior high school students spending the majority of their weeknights logged into graphical chat rooms and IM services via 56K dial-up lines. In the four years or so that's since passed, DSL and cable modems have become commonplace in businesses, schools, and hi-tech American households, and those same kids are getting ready to go off to college where, no doubt, some of them will begin engineering the technology that will push the information revolution into its next phase. They've already learned the basics of HTML and even Java programming in high school, remember. These disciplines didn't even exist less than twenty years ago when they were born.

THE PROMISE OF THE INTERNET FOR
TEACHING AND LEARNING

This chapter has given a brief overview of the historical landscape from which the Internet has risen. From the printing press to the personal computer, the technology of communication has changed quite a bit since the days of Johannes Gutenberg, and it has been progressing most rapidly over the past half century. One thing that hasn't changed during all that time, though, is our desire and ability to communicate our thoughts, opinions, and desires to one another. Whether it's through handwritten letters or emoticons typed into chat rooms, human beings are social creatures, and we yearn to share with one other what is going on in our hearts and our heads.[5]

Education is largely about understanding. We strive to understand new mathematic principles and scientific laws. We read and write literature in the ongoing attempt to share and understand the variety of human experiences. We study history and anthropology to better understand societies and their historical roles in the evolution of the world. The Internet promises much for communication, and with that, much for education and understanding at large.

What makes the Internet so unique and powerful is the ability it lends individuals to research and broadcast information with a minimum of physical effort and invested time. Access to high-speed connections and improved usability will only get better as time goes on. When taken in the long view, the Net as we now know it is only in its nascent stage. Even still, a simple text query of a web-based search engine will provide dozens of links to resources on a given topic within seconds. Those links, when effectively screened and employed, can mark the beginning of a foray into a virtual spider's web of knowledge stemming from a single topic. A search for "baseball" can lead to player statistics, mathematical disciplines, and foundations of calculus just as easily as it could lead to Jackie Robinson, civil rights, or this year's divisional play-off winners.

The amount of useful information available online grows with each passing hour, and will only grow faster as access is brought to more and more of the world's population—all of this at our fingertips and soon in the palms of our hands wherever we go. To paraphrase the electronic musician D. J. Shadow, "The Entire Canon" of recorded thought—or close to it—is online, and the collection is growing by the minute.[6] The chapters that follow will take a look at how the Internet is changing teaching and learning and how it will continue to do so in the future. Though the majority of the experiences drawn from and presented here deal with classroom teaching and learning on the K–12 level, my aim is to provide ideas and insights that can be helpful to anyone wanting to use the Internet to better teach with and learn from.

My guiding philosophy is a simple one: The Internet, and the computers we use to access it, are tools like any other. No tool should ever take the place of a teacher, but rather it is the teacher's job to learn to effectively integrate tools into his or her methodologies. Children should learn to use a computer and learn to research online. They also should learn to read, write, and speak effectively, work and play with others, and negotiate a world in which people matter above and beyond all else—science and technology included.

Learning to use a PC and the Internet may be a more expansive, ever-shifting task than learning to use the Dewey decimal system that governs your city or school's library, but the two goals are on par with one another. The Net is an amazing tool for research and collaboration. Its almost-real-time growth, which can be daunting, is one of the Net's greatest attributes.

The future of the Internet's impact on education lies in the ability of teachers and students to use it for effective research and collaboration. It's just as easy for a student to spend all evening using the Net to research scientific principles or baseball scores as it is for that student to hang out in a chat room. All three activities have their merits, yet then it becomes the role of the teacher not only to teach the basic skills necessary for students to make use of the technology but also to guide those students toward constructive, engaging uses of the information that the technology puts at their disposal. The trick, especially with young learners, is often to hook onto something they're already interested in and relate new material to that. Thankfully, the Net and web in particular are aptly named; for every topic available online, there is a link or series of links leading straight to almost every other topic. Learning to work the web as a spider would, and not getting trapped in one corner of it like a hapless fly, is the key.

It is my sincere hope that this book will inspire you to explore, experiment with, and challenge the ideas that you encounter within. Education is about communication and understanding, and there is work involved in each. Only through taking what a teacher has shown him or her and applying that to the unique experiences and principles of his or her own life can a student really begin to learn.

NOTES

1. The Chinese invented rag paper in or around 105 C.E. The technology was passed on to Arabs in the eighth century but did not make its way to the Europeans until several hundred years later, in the twelfth and thirteenth centuries. From http://www.digitalcentury.com/encyclopedia/print.html

2. http://www.digitalcentury.com/encyclopedia/print.html

3. http://www.digitalcentury.com/encyclopedia/print.html

4. For more, see suggested reading list that follows.

5. An emoticon is a group of ASCII characters that, when viewed sideways, form a facial expression. For example :-) is a smile ;-) is a wink :-o is an open-mouthed look of surprise, and so on. Emoticons have become common parlance in chat rooms, instant messages, and e-mails over the past few years.

6. D. J. Shadow, a 21st-century recording artist who specializes in electronically combining and remixing prerecorded music from various genres to come up with his own style of hip hop-cum-dance music, was once asked about the influences on his compositional style. He replied that "the entire canon of recorded music" was his biggest influence because technology allows him to draw upon any and every bit of recorded sound he could find when working on a new song.

SUGGESTED READING

Walter Benjamin, *Walter Benjamin: Selected Writings* (Cambridge, Mass.: Belknap Press, 1996–). This multivolume set contains the seminal essay "The Work of Art in the Age of Mechanical Reproduction," 1935.

———, *Illuminations*, edited and with an introduction by Hannah Arendt; translated by Harry Zohn (New York: Shocken Books, 1985).

Judy Breck, *The Wireless Age: Its Meaning for Learning and Schools* (Lanham, Md.: ScarecrowEducation, 2001).

Sebastian de Assis, *Revolution in Education* (Lanham, Md.: ScarecrowEducation, 2002).

Fredric Jameson, *Postmodernism, or the Cultural Logic of Late Capitalism* (Durham, N.C.: Duke University Press, 1992).

Marshall McLuhan, *The Gutenberg Galaxy* (Toronto, Ontario: University of Toronto Press, 1962).

———, *Essential McLuhan*, edited by Eric McLuhan and Frank Zingrone (New York: Basic Books, 1995).

Marshall McLuhan and Quentin Fiore, *The Medium Is the Massage* (Ginko Press, 2001).

Lorenzo Charles Simpson, *Technology, Time, and the Conversations of Modernity* (New York: Routledge, 1995).

Charles K. Stallard, *The Promise of Technology in Schools: The Next 20 Years* (Lanham, Md.: ScarecrowEducation, 2002).

SUGGESTED VIEWING

Startup.com, Jehane Noujaim and Chris Hegedus, directors (Artisan Entertainment, 2001). Available on DVD.

Chapter Two

Trust the Children, Teach the Children

MAKING SENSE OF THE WORLD AROUND YOU

Computers are here to stay, and it is vital that we weave them into the ways we teach and learn, much as we have started to do with the ways we communicate and do business. Computer-based learning is paramount to the future of our schools, but never at the expense of increased teacher recruitment, training, and professional development.

Technology should not and will not ever take the place of teachers; computers are tools just like pencils, paper, and textbooks. To that end, they are tools that are now a part of our everyday world. Furthermore, computer skills are expected of job seekers and come in quite handy in a growing variety of situations in both the world outside of school and the world inside academia. Public and private schools in America are pouring more and more time and money into computer equipment, and in short course we have started to see those resources being deployed more effectively.

Schools and individual educators have a responsibility to their students to stay abreast of learning technologies and integrate those that will aid the learning process. Sometimes this means sticking with years-old methods, and other times this means updating tools and methodologies, if not the curricula and pedagogies themselves. The field of educational technology has advanced itself far enough at the beginning of the 21st century to show that computers, particularly those equipped for Internet access, are a worthwhile investment for most teachers and learners in most fields of study at most levels.

Most? Why only most?

Children these days often have computers in their homes or have fairly easy access to computers and other pervasive technologies (television and videos, video games, for example) elsewhere. If they show an interest in learning more about technology on their own or if their parents want to get them on the machines at a young age, that's fine. But there is absolutely no need for time to be taken away from the critical processes of socialization, group cooperation, and basic skill development in favor of additional time with technology before the age of eight or nine.

If technology can be woven into early elementary classrooms as a useful aid to the larger goals of the cognitive and social development of students—and it certainly can and has been already by many a thoughtful, creative educator—that's great. But children who don't spend a great deal of time behind a monitor and keyboard before junior high school aren't in great danger of being left for dead at the side of the information superhighway, either.

For all of their usefulness, computers can have a dark side of fostering isolationism in certain situations (as will be discussed later). Ours is a social world, and part of the reason for sending children to school, on play dates, and to other group activities is to foster the healthy social skills necessary for navigating a world shared with other people. In no way will a child be at a disadvantage for not having received formal training on computers or other technology before age eight, and that's a conservative appraisal. Kids at this age shouldn't necessarily be kept away from computers, but they shouldn't be forced to sit in front of them, either. Their focus should be on growing comfortable with the social and physical realities of the world, not to mention the basics of reading, writing, and arithmetic.[1]

In the same way that a child raised in a bilingual household will naturally grow to speak both languages, so too are today's children learning the ins and outs of PCs, cell phones, video games, and other gadgets as a natural part of their being raised in a technological society. Children are amazingly adaptive, resourceful learners. Technology is part of the world we have created for them, and they grow up learning to use it.

I have taught third graders to use personal computers and I have tutored fifty-year-old-adults with Ph.D.s and intellectually challenging occupations to use the same personal computers. Of course there are always quick studies and slow learners; much as I'll never be a professional gymnast, some people just don't have a good feel for the way computers work. But, by and large, the kids just get it faster than the adults do.

Maybe it's because adults try to reason their way through things while kids just dive right in and give it a go. Maybe it's because adults can remember when computers were giant, scary behemoths born out of top-secret research labs, and kids today are introduced to computing by way of candy-colored plastic orbs with their own pet mice nestled on desks in the bedroom and kitchen.

Whatever the case, I've never seen a nine-year-old try to master the basics of running a computer application by writing down step-by-step directions, whereas several of the adults I've worked with do just that for every new task they encounter. Children are much more likely to simply keep asking how to, say, "get KidPix to work" until they remember how to get KidPix to work. (KidPix is a popular multimedia program used at many elementary and middle schools.) Soon enough, the principle of looking in the "Programs" folder for the KidPix icon and double-clicking it is transferred to getting Word (or whatever other application they want) to work.

The child may not know that he is taking a specific skill and learning to apply it to different contexts, but that is just what he is doing. The adult learner may well be stuck with her notebook full of step-by-step instructions for accessing each of the dozen applications on her computer.

People tend to learn best when they can lend context to a skill or task, and kids are no exception to this rule. Ask an English student to write a sentence that demonstrates the rules for serial comma usage and you may well get a blank stare. Ask that same student, if she's a basketball fan, to write a sentence listing several of Michael Jordan's attributes while being careful about her commas, and you're more likely to get what you're after: Michael Jordan is the greatest basketball player of all time, a global marketing icon, and a very wealthy man.

We must constantly navigate our world, acquire new skills for new situations, and update our strategies and methodologies as things change in and around our lives. Children are both less experienced with the world and less set in their ways than adults, and so they tend to run on autopilot a little less often than grownups, and more actively seek out new patterns and relationships to make sense of what they encounter.

The computer is based on rigid laws of logic—cute icons and seemingly random system crashes notwithstanding. These laws encourage the sorts of pattern and context seeking in which child learners in particular intuitively excel. Perhaps, for all the intricacy of the programming languages and operating systems, using a computer generally boils down to one golden rule: Remember which buttons and menus control which functions and the computer does what you want it to.

IMMERSING YOURSELF IN A NEW LANGUAGE

Language is our primary tool for making sense of the world and communicating that sense with others. The definition of language can be extended to encompass many forms: written, spoken, visual, musical, and so on. Using a personal computer or other instrument of digital technology requires understanding an entirely new language.

At one end of the spectrum is the language that breathes life into the beast itself, the binary code of ones and zeros that all machine language is, at its core, broken into. These switches have only two states and even the most complex matrix of circuitry is built from these simple on/off gates. More user-friendly programming languages have developed over the past half-century so, but even today's popular flavors like Java and C++ must be compiled into "machine language" (another name for binary code) before a computer can make sense of them. Of course, user-friendliness is a relative state of mind: While binary code isn't seen as very friendly by all but the most practiced scientist, Java and C++ are still far worse than Greek to the layperson.

At the other end of the computer user's linguistic spectrum lies a more common and more metaphorical language. The systems of icons and text labels, mouse clicks, and keystrokes that most home and business computer users rely on today—Windows and Mac OS being the most popular—are indeed languages unto themselves even if we don't usually think of them that way. The "picture that you click on to get to the word program" has a proper name and context in which it should correctly be used: double-click the *icon* to launch Microsoft Word. Syntax is important when navigating a PC's operating system, as is sequence; just as switching the order of the subject and predicate muddles the sense of a sentence, so too does reversing the sequence of highlight and double-click make that darned computer do just what you *didn't* want it to do . . . again.

KNOWING HOW AND WHERE TO LOOK

Just as one can pick up enough French or Italian to make rudimentary sense of the language (a tourist's sense, anyway) without understanding its grammatical particulars, many a computer user gets his machine to behave without really understanding the logical underpinnings of its system of commands. This is fine for limited usage, but is also symptomatic of those folks who write down step-by-step instructions for everything they want the machine to do instead of, say, understanding that the menu bars are universal and context-sensitive. That is, whether you're running Microsoft Word or Adobe Photoshop, you'll still see a menu bar with some choices common to both programs ("File," "Edit," "View," "Window," "Help") and others that are specific to each program (Word has "Format" and "Font" where Photoshop has "Image," "Layer," and "Filter").

To the novice—or nervous—user, this knowledge seems too complicated; he just wants to know how to type something and save it, or what the step-by-step instructions are for getting a picture off the digital camera and printing it. The savvy user knows that understanding the commonalities of the language under different contexts is both easier and more helpful than memorizing task-specific directives. Learning how the system works in a broad sense enables you to predict how individual programs will function. Common commands reside in familiar places and new ones are uncovered because you know how and where to look for them.

This, in many ways, is what digital technology in the age of the Internet is about: knowing how and where to look. With so many resources at your fingertips today, it's not as much about knowing things as it's about knowing where to find them. Shameful as it is to say, I cannot name all of the past presidents of the United States. Give me a computer with a decent Net connection, though, and I can find them, along with their dates in office and relevant personal data, faster than you can recite their names from memory.

People I've taught or watched learn to use a personal computer tend to learn by intuition, trial, and error as much as by studying rules or memorizing commands. Studying and memorizing are, of course, important parts of attaining mastery of many things. But as is also the case with most things, having motivation to study makes all the difference in the world.

The classes I've taught to use computers, be they third graders or third-grade teachers, always featured a few novices, a few experts, and a lot of in-betweeners. The students who come in as novices in September and leave as experts in June are generally the ones who are able to grasp the contextual underpinnings of how the computer works. Through trial and error, immersing themselves in the material, and feeling their way through it toward comprehension, they assimilate more than they memorize the ways in which different functions of the machine relate to one another.

Maybe an accidental click of the right-side mouse button reveals an unexpected window of commands, and subsequent trials of this technique show that right-clicking always yields this contextual menu of options. Maybe being taught to open a sound file by dragging it to the music player application doesn't readily translate to an abstraction but eventually leads to the student wanting to know what happens when, say, he drags a downloaded picture onto the Adobe Photoshop icon. Whether the words are there to describe it or not, the student has assimilated the idea that files can be opened with specific applications by dragging icons atop other icons.

Immersing students in a new world and giving them the freedom and responsibility of feeling their way around it can be an effective way of introducing complicated new material such as a foreign language. I'm not talking about pushing the boy off the pier without a life preserver so he'll learn to swim, but rather arming students with basic skills and knowledge and then letting them try to figure things out for themselves before bombarding them with laminated sheets of rules and regulations.

Learning should come and go hand in hand with a sense of accomplishment and pride on the learner's part. Learning from someone else's experience is an effective way to quickly learn proper technique, and there is often no better substitute for it. Learning by figuring something out on one's own, though, can be an immensely satisfying process, one that encourages further exploration and growth.[2]

Rather than teach your students all of the basics of using a computer, why not teach them a few things and then give them a checklist of tasks to try to figure out on their own? Make sure students have mastered the basics of whatever environment they're working in (this idea works better with something like basic pointing-and-clicking or web browsing than it does with advanced Java programming, obviously) and keep the list to a handful of items.

Try this mini lesson plan covering the basics of using the Mac or Windows operating system (OS) with beginning students of any age. You may wish to shorten the lesson or explain things more thoroughly to younger students:

Lesson #1: Operating System Basics

Objective: To familiarize students with the basics of manipulating files and objects in the operating system and using the menu bar to access program functionality; to address the concept of context-specific menu bars across different computer applications and to encourage students to explore unfamiliar applications through the menu bars.

Age Level: Third grade through adult

Skill Level: Beginner

Time Required: 15–40 minutes, depending on age

Materials Needed: Computers running Mac OS or Windows

Note: This lesson plan has been written for Mac OS X but can be adapted for whatever flavor of the Mac or Windows operating system you are using. The basics of icons, menu bars, and file management are similar enough to allow for easy translation to the operating system of your choosing. In Windows, an "alias" is referred to as a "shortcut," and the application "Text edit" is "Notepad." There is no direct Windows equivalent of the Macintosh "Finder," but for these purposes you can think of the Finder as a basic application screen without any files selected or open (i.e., Microsoft Word running without any Word documents actually open).

Prepare the computers so that each one has a shortcut to "Text Edit" (Notepad) on the desktop along with the hard drive and a file called "sample.txt" that was created in Text Edit. The file should have two or three paragraphs of dummy text for the students to manipulate later in the lesson.

Assign one computer to each student or group of students. This lesson is based around hands-on usage of the system and so works best with no more than two students to a computer.

From within the "Finder" (Mac OS), explain the basics of icons and menu bars. Make sure students understand that each icon on the desktop represents one element within the operating system, be it a disk, folder, file, application, or printer (or alias pointing to any of the above). Ask students to guess at why different elements are graphically represented as they are and explain how different elements are meant to look different for easy identification.

Show students the menu bar at the top of the screen and explain that this bar is almost always present when using the computer. Depending on what application you are running, the choices on the bar change. Take them through the Finder's menu bar selections by having them single-click on each of the choices (Finder, File, Edit, View, Go, Window, Help) to reveal the drop-down menus. Explain that they can always look at the drop-down menus to see most of the options available to them within an application.

Explain to students that in order to perform any action on an element you must first single-click it, which highlights the icon. Ask students to single-click "sample.txt" and then choose "Get Info" from the File menu. Ask them to look in the resulting information window to find out what program was used to create this file.

Have students guess what program will be used to open this file, and then double-click the file to open it. The file should open in Text Edit.

Explain to the students that Text Edit allows them to perform basic formatting on text. Tell them that in order to manipulate text they must first highlight the text and then use the drop-down menus. Show them how to highlight text. (If anyone asks about the icon-based toolbar, you can explain that it replicates the functionality of the drop-down menus.)

Assign a handful of simple formatting tasks to perform on the text in the file—depending on your available time, you might give them anywhere from a few to a dozen tasks of varying difficulty. Tasks should include those that use the Edit menu (cutting, pasting, copying, and spell-checking text) and the Format menu (changing the size, font face, and style of the text). Do *not* give the students step-by-step instructions, but rather encourage them to explore the drop-down menus.

When finished, students should use the File menu to save their work and then quit Text Edit.

Students should then go back to the Finder and use the Finder's drop-down menus to duplicate their file, move the duplicate to the trash, and empty the trash. Again, do not explain how to perform these tasks beyond pointing out that the menu bar can be used to access all necessary functions.

Extra-Credit: If time permits, have students repeat the above exercise using keystroke commands instead of the drop-down menus. Explain that many menu bar functions can be performed from the keyboard using combinations of keystrokes. See if students can figure out how to do this and also move from icon to icon on the desktop using the letter and arrow keys.

This lesson is not a complicated one, but is a great way to introduce students to using a personal computer. From the beginning, students should understand how today's computers are designed to provide context-specific information and functionality. This knowledge will help them to explore areas of interest on their own and learn advanced techniques within programs that interest them. This concept of knowing where to look (both in new situations and when one can't recall a specific command) will benefit students throughout their use of computers and provide a basis for learning to use the Internet.

Encouraging students to learn on their own through exploration will also benefit you as much as it will them. Many students are more than happy to share newfound knowledge with their peers, especially when the entire class is first charting their way through new waters. From my own experience, I can tell you that having a few quick learners willing to help out their peers can make a world of difference when it comes to trying to teach and manage a computer lab full of novice computer users.

A MUSEUM GUIDE ON THE INTERNET

During my junior year of college, I had the fortune of taking a course on the literature of James Joyce. My professor was a great Joycean scholar and an even bigger fan—his love of the subject matter shone through in every class meeting. The course was his favorite to teach and turned out to be one of my favorites to have taken as an undergraduate.

During one of the first class meetings, our professor said something that has stuck with me to this day (long since my understanding of the nuances of *Ulysses* left me): "When teaching literature, I like to think of myself as a museum guide," he told us. "I am here to lead you through the material, pointing out areas of particular interest to which I'd like you to pay careful attention, guiding you toward other areas you might not have noticed on your own, and answering questions you might have along the way. You will discover things I wasn't yet aware of, I am sure, and any questions that I don't have the answers to, I promise to research before our next meeting."

While this ideology might prove a bit more effective with college students than third graders, the notion of "educator as museum guide" is one that I have tried to apply to all of my teaching endeavors. When thinking about using the Internet in education, this is a particularly useful strategy to employ.

The world is made up of individuals. The Internet is made up of the online activity of individuals. Individuals are, by definition, unique, but they also seek out like-minded counterparts with whom to form communities and work as groups. The web is much the same—individuals create web pages and form communities and companies with which to build larger, more complicated websites. Search engines and directories lump similar websites together so they may be found more easily, webmasters form webrings to drive traffic between linked websites, and like-minded individuals form listservs, BBSs, and other online communities to share knowledge and experiences.

What makes the Internet such an innovative and exciting medium is the ease with which individuals can broadcast information to one another. Print, radio, and television make it easy for individuals to receive information, but unless you have some pretty hefty resources behind you it's difficult to broadcast a message to the masses through one of these channels. Radio and television transmitters (let alone broadcast licenses) are prohibitively expensive, and while a printed manifesto can be copied on the cheap, getting it out to a large group of people still requires lots money, lots of legwork, or both.

The Internet is changing all of that. With an initial investment in a computer, access to the Net, and some time to learn the basics, almost anyone can create and post a web page (or send an e-mail) that can be viewed by the rest of the world. Getting the word out is still an issue (if a story about a tree falling is posted on a web page deep in cyberspace, will anyone read it?) but the ease with which e-mails are forwarded and mass-mailed has made word-of-mouth and "guerilla" marketing more powerful than ever. As such, information is being broadcast, viewed, commented upon, and rebroadcast like never before, all by way of the Net. The result is a wealth of information on almost every topic under the sun, right at your fingertips, and most of it is available for free.

Of course, not all of the information available online is accurate or verifiable. We have come, as a society, to trust certain authorities as our purveyors of truth: television and radio networks, newspapers, and books written by expert authors and distributed by name-brand publishing houses. The accuracy of the versions of the truth disseminated by these sources and the interests they represent is a debate for another time and place.[3] However, these larger broadcasters are subject to more stringent laws and regulations than individual webcasters, and so we tend to place our faith in them when it comes to reporting the news on a national level.

Still, whether you're looking at cnn.com or the neighborhood gossip e-mail newsletter, it's up to you to filter the truth from what you see and hear online. As an educator, your responsibility extends to your students as well. Depending on their age and experience, your job lies somewhere between acting as a content filter and teaching them media literacy skills so that they can learn for themselves how to separate fact from fiction.

Thinking of the Net as a giant online museum, then, your role is in fact that of a museum guide. Whatever the subject to be explored, you are likely to be more informed than your students on some aspects of it, less informed on others, and armed with your own agenda to offer up during the day's exploration of the museum. Additionally, you hope not only to point students to what they need in order to realize that agenda, but also to show them new things they might wish to explore further on their own.

Like a museum, the Net is there to be visited again and again, with or without a tour guide to show you around. And, like good museums, the Net has the resources to grab its visitors' attention and keep them coming back for more. When you use the Internet in your classroom, the context you provide for your students makes it "your" Internet—therefore, it's up to you to provide the resources necessary to get your students interested in using the Net for constructive, educational purposes and to keep them coming back on their own to explore and construct "their" Internet.

GUIDELINES FOR SAFE SURFING

In a perfect world, there would be no need to protect our children from those with whom they share the planet. Parents and teachers would educate and guide the young, helping them to make sense of what they encounter and encouraging them to learn from and share with the other people in the world. People would help and not harm one another.

Unfortunately, we all know this isn't the case. Our world isn't perfect, but it is pretty good. Still, parents can't keep an eye on their children all day, nor can they know all of what their kids are exposed to in daily life and by the media. Similarly, teachers can't be expected to keep tabs on what all of their students are doing at all times during a class period. This is perhaps even more true in a computer lab than in a traditional classroom setting—many computer labs are set up so that students are facing both their monitors and teachers. Great for learning, not so great for teachers who want to monitor students' onscreen activities.

There are those among us—politicians and talk show hosts, most noticeably—who would have you believe that the Internet has given rise to the spread of evil over the past decade or so. There are things online that many of us wish weren't there: violent imagery, hateful propaganda, plans for bomb building, and so on. Well, the Internet didn't give birth to these things. Their existence is a fact of life, as is the reality that the Internet is a very accessible form of mass communication, governed in America by the same First Amendment protection of free speech as everything else you say and write.

There will always be certain websites and chat-room postings you wish weren't there for your students to stumble upon. There will be lies disguised as truth, opinion disguised as fact, and hate mongering disguised as advertising potholing the road to educational exploration. This is no different from the rest of real life, except that life on the screen is a faster, more time-condensed experience than much of what we call "real life."

That is to say that just as one of the great things about the Net is the ease and speed with which you can use it to learn, one of the potential pitfalls of life online is the ease and speed with which you can find yourself caught in an unsavory web of pop-up ads, obscene text and images, and other online places you'd rather not be exposed to.

So as an educator responsible for the mental growth of your students, what can you do to protect them without censoring their learning?

FILTERING SOFTWARE IS NO SUBSTITUTE FOR TALKING

In the academic year 2000–2001, 1,066,945 elementary and secondary students attended New York City public schools.[4] The New York City Department of Education (NYCDOE, formerly known as the New York City Board of Education) filters all web content provided to its schools. A student browsing a website from an NYCDOE computer lab will see that site only after its content has been checked by a central server running software that performs two main tasks. First, the URL (uniform resource locator) of the website is checked against a master list of blocked domains. If the URL is on the list, the user gets an error message explaining that the site is blocked and will not be shown. A reason or explanation is also given, detailing which category of prohibited material the offending site fell under.

For instance, the AOL Instant Messenger home page at http://www.aim.com is banned because that page falls under the "Chat/Interactive" category and students are not allowed into unmonitored chat rooms and bulletin board systems on school property. Pornography sites are blocked because minors are not legally allowed to view them. Certain sports and entertainment sites are blocked because they have been deemed inappropriate for in-school viewing. The list goes on.

If a page makes it through the list of blocked domains, it is then subjected to content-filtering software that scans the body text of the page for inappropriate content. The software uses criteria approved by the NYCDOE to tally up a score based on the frequency of offensive words and questionable content on a given web page. Any page whose score exceeds a certain threshold is blocked from being viewed. This second line of defense is meant to filter out inappropriate material that slips through the list of blocked domains. Simply put, there are too many offensive websites out there to keep track of, so a quick scan for dirty words should do the trick.

During the academic years 1997 to 1999, the private school in Brooklyn that I taught at had a K–12 enrollment of under 1,000 students. This school did not use filtering software on the two dozen online computers available to students in the main computer lab. Security software was installed to keep students from accessing system settings (NYCDOE employs similar software, as should most computer labs these days) but no Internet content filtering was done by the school. Instead, students were informed of which websites were off limits in the lab—usually by way of the lab coordinator saying something like, "No AOL, guys"—and anyone caught in restricted territory was barred from the lab for a spell, given detention, or both.

Both policies work, and both have their flaws. Both are also very context specific. The NYCDOE system sometimes unintentionally blocks websites that have solid educational value and makes it hard for teachers to use certain web-based e-mail systems. I myself have been unable to read perfectly chaste e-mails on NYCDOE computers because of some quirk or another in the filtering software. But when you're legally responsible for keeping over a million students out of harm's way, you do what you have to do. In 21st-century America, it's very easy to sue someone else for a perceived wrongdoing; the department of education can't afford to let its students see photographs of naked people on a school-owned computer screen.

The private school's system does allow for the occasional clandestine foray into a chat room or viewing of unclothed tribesmen on *National Geographic*'s website, but it also allows for the academic freedom and intellectual exploration that the school prides itself on. With such a small student body and very manageable computer lab, it's easy to keep tabs on students. The students know they're being trusted to play by the rules, so they generally do. When they don't, word spreads quickly from the lab to the main office to Mom and/or Dad. When students question the authority standing between them and using the computer lab for online chatting, they are generally met with a reasonable explanation and thoughtful discussion of the matter.

This kind of a policy simply wouldn't work in a public school system that gives thousands of teachers responsibility for groups of about thirty students each, all across the five boroughs of New York City. In either case, I would hope that a student who genuinely wants to know why she's being banned from certain places on the Internet is afforded the chance to discuss the matter with her teachers or principal.

Freedom of speech has always been something of a tricky matter for American citizens and lawmakers, and the extension of this constitutional right into cyberspace only promises more interesting, controversial, and policy-shifting debates in years to come. Today's children are tomorrow's leaders, or so I've always been told, and it is at least as important to explain to them why they're being protected from something as it is to protect them from it in the first place.

Educators are not naïve to the legal, political, and moral implications of letting students have access to what society at large deems "inappropriate material." This is particularly true in the case of adults teaching children. Children, particularly those growing up in urban environments, come in contact with the best and worst that the "real world" has to offer on a daily basis. We would like for school to be something of a safe haven for them—not an escape from the truths of the world, but rather a place for them to learn about and discuss right and wrong and ultimately begin their lives' work of making the world a better place in which to live.

Definitions of "education," "right," and "wrong" are as many and varied as the people who write them. One man's virtue is another man's vice and so on. Since the nature of group education is to bring a collection of individuals, no matter their ages or backgrounds, together for the purpose of learning about something, the educator must be tolerant and respectful of his students' many values and points of view. When the individuals in question are children attending public schools, the educator's job is expanded to not only respect his students, but also to pay heed to the points of view of those students' parents and guardians. This is where things get tricky.

Filtering software is a real-world solution for the problem facing schools that rightly believe the Internet is a necessary tool for today's students. School faculty and administrators need to negotiate waters fraught with parents, politicians, and others who believe children should be kept away from a portion of what the Net has to offer. As with anything else, district and school technology personnel need to learn the ins and outs of filtering software before installing or deploying it.

Remember, though, that education—like life—is about learning to make sense of facts and figures, people, and points of view. If your school is employing filtering software, look at it as a chance to open up discussions with your students about such topics as freedom of speech and the international nature of the Internet and cyberspace law. There's plenty of good content out there on the web and Net at large; if one good resource is blocked from access, chances are there's a decent substitute available for the finding. If not, there's always the option of teaching your students about lobbying and petitioning the powers that be for change.

THREE Rs AND AN S?

My high school guidance counselor once told me that no matter what other courses I took before graduation, I had to take typing. Whether I became a doctor, lawyer, teacher, or writer, being able to type would come in handier than I could imagine.

Little did he know how wise his words were; with each day that passes, the amount of time I spend using my computer seems to increase. Writing, communicating via e-mail, surfing the web, researching on the Net, composing music and burning it to CDs, my laptop has literally become the hub of my working life, and a core part of my creative and social lives as well. I can't imagine how many letters and words I tap on its keyboard in a given day, but I do know that if I hadn't learned to type I'd probably spend even more time behind the screen than I do now. And as much as the computer lets me do, there's plenty of life calling me from beyond the screen.

The 21st-century version of the "learn to type" mantra for high schoolers should be updated to read "learn to type and surf the web." We've all heard of the "three Rs"—reading, 'riting, and 'rithmetic. I now humbly offer an addendum to the troika that has guided American education for the past century: an S. Schoolchildren should learn to surf. Any student learning to use a computer, child or adult, should learn to surf. I hope that good, old-fashioned libraries with their dusty stacks of reference books and heavy wooden tables full of intense-looking strangers hunkered over old periodicals never go away, but the truth is that learning to effectively surf the web is a more valuable skill in today's world than knowing how to decipher the Dewey decimal system.

Knowing how to surf the web, of course, is no replacement for knowing how to read, write, and add numbers together. Just as the computer is no replacement for a good teacher, learning to use a computer to find information is not a substitute for learning the basic skills that are still essential to getting along in life. Rather, using a computer has become another important skill to be learned in school. Computers can help us perform complex tasks, but we still must know how to solve problems in order to program a computer to do the grunt work involved in finding solutions. As the old adage goes, "Garbage in, garbage out." In other words, if you don't know what you're asking the computer to do for you, don't expect it to get much done.

The chapters that follow will explore in more depth the dual role that the computer can play in helping you both acquire and share knowledge—experiencing and constructing the Internet, if you will. Every educational experience enhanced by technology is a chance to learn about how technology works, and also to think about what the role of technology is and should be in a particular field of study.

While a computer could be worked into almost any educational foray in one way or another, it is important to think about whether the time spent using technology is worth what it lends to accomplishing the task at hand. Within that examination comes a look at a perhaps more important, if ultimately less answerable, question: What is the purpose of education? A question asked throughout the ages, but one no less important in today's complex and fragmented yet interdependent and webbed world—what is the point of educating ourselves and our children? Certainly it isn't only about standardized tests and the status quo.

With technology providing more opportunities for customized learning and individual exploration than ever before, and the Internet promising to bring those opportunities to more people than ever before, it is well worth our time to pause for a moment and consider what it is that we are trying to teach and what we hope to learn from one another.

NOTES

1. Home schooling is not a topic on which I am qualified to speak at any length. The ideas presented here are based on my experiences with and research

on group learning. Suffice it to say that, in my opinion, learning to function as part of a group is an important aspect of the education of any individual. Later sections of the book will consider the benefits of technology to independent learning, which is a vital component of education as well and perhaps more applicable to home schooling.

2. John Dewey is often cited as one of the fathers of progressive, experiential education. His pedagogical philosophy centered around the idea that there literally is no substitute for experience. See the following suggested reading list.

3. The collected writings of Noam Chomsky are a good starting point for a radical perspective on the forces at work behind corporate media. See the suggested reading list.

4. Data according to the National Center for Educational Statistics, taken from http://nces.ed.gov/pubs2002/2002351.pdf in spring 2003.

SUGGESTED READING

Judy Breck, *How We Will Learn in the 21st Century* (Lanham, Md.: Scarecrow-Education, 2002).

Noam Chomsky, *The Chomsky Reader*, edited by James Peck (New York: Pantheon Books, 1987).

Noam Chomsky and Edward S. Herman, *Manufacturing Consent: The Political Economy of the Mass Media* (New York: Pantheon Books, 2002).

John Dewey, *Experience and Education* (New York: Free Press, 1997).

Chapter Three

Context Is Everything: Experience, Understand, Build

DIGITAL SKILLS ARE REAL WORLD SKILLS

There is an opportunity for learning in everything that we do throughout the course of a day. Doing something new, like learning to ride a bike, is obviously a learning experience. But even the most seemingly mundane activity is a chance for learning. Yoga teachers, for instance, coach their students to be aware of their breathing at all times throughout a given pose or movement because yogis believe there is much to be learned through the simplest acts, if they are done with great care. Often it is, in fact, the things we are most accustomed to doing that present the greatest opportunities for learning. The trick is get ourselves to open up and pay attention to what we're actually doing instead of just going through the motions.

In this book, we are learning to better use the Internet and digital technology in education, not mastering yoga poses. However, the guiding philosophy of opening ourselves up to new chances for learning remains true whether one is in "child's pose" or sitting at the computer. This is particularly so when learning to surf the web and using the Internet in general, because everything that we encounter online was built by someone somewhere, and it is the nature of technology that these things will eventually be replaced by newly evolved versions of themselves.

Whether you are teaching math, science, literature, or history, whenever you work with students in a particular subject area you are actually touching upon several disciplines at once. Students of any subject must know not only the specifics of their specialty but also the more general practices of conducting research, organizing and communicating information, and using critical thinking skills to evaluate findings. Although the particulars of these skills vary depending on the subject matter (the calculus student is naturally less concerned with the rules governing sentence structure than the literature student is), the threads running through the basics of working with information are common to all disciplines.

Information technology is a term commonly applied to computer-specific trades. However, the science of information technology extends to almost every facet of modern life. The development of machine-aided methods for processing and representing data is big business. It is also at the heart of our society's progress since the invention of the printing press, and over the past half-century in particular.

Have you paid bills online without having written a check or licking a stamp? Have you found yourself amazed by a supermarket clerk who can carry on a conversation with you while he rings up groceries without looking, using the computerized scanner? Does it make you happy that even though your local branch of the public library doesn't have the book you're looking for, they can get it from the next town within the week? You have information technology to thank for all of those scenarios, to name just a few.

When thinking about leveraging the Internet to aid whatever subject you teach, remember that you are not only enhancing your students' learning of that subject matter, you are also furthering their mastery of information technology skills that are fast becoming essential to daily life.

Learning to work a mouse, send a word-processing document via e-mail, create a web page, and even stream live video across the globe: not long ago we viewed these tasks as magic tricks performed exclusively by scientists, and now they are the concrete skills we expect of our peers in social and working life. Fast-food workers have to be able to use digital cash registers and order delivery systems; employers expect their office workers to be experienced with e-mail, voice mail, word processing, and databases; academics must know LexisNexis as well as they do the Dewey decimal system. This isn't magic; these are real-world skills for today's real life.

Whether you use the Internet on a regular basis in your classroom or bring your students to the computer lab only once in a while for research and special activities, why not equip them with a solid foundation of technology skills upon which they might build on their own or in more specialized courses of study? In chapter two I suggested a lesson on getting a handle on the basics of the computer's operating system. Now let's move on to some basic but very practical skills to help students utilize the world of information technology available to them.

SMART SEARCHING IS SMOOTH SURFING

The World Wide Web is the most easily accessible part of the Internet. Web pages provide a standardized way for people to publish and retrieve information to and from almost anywhere in the world. Learning to use search engines is at the heart of making effective use of the World Wide Web. There is an important distinction to be made between an educated adult using a search engine as a starting point for research and a teacher turning her class of junior high school students loose on Google.com.

Effective web searching presupposes a level of critical thinking that enables you to differentiate valid information from rumors and opinion, and truth from lies. Furthermore, much of the information on the web is text, but the reading level at which it is written can vary greatly from source to source. Search engines generally don't sort results according to the comprehension level required to decipher the information on a page, so a certain level of "information literacy" must be achieved in order to weed out useful search results from the junk.

The concept behind search engines is simple: Databases logging as much of the content on the web as possible are attached to web pages designed to field your queries, cross-check them with the logged information, and return the results. In other words, you can go to a search page and enter "French restaurants in New York City." The page will feed your search criteria into the database, and any logged websites containing those words (French restaurants in New York City) will be returned. Actually, any websites containing *any* of those words (except *in*, because search engines ignore common words such as *in*, *an*, *the*) will be returned, ranked in order of relevance from exact to partial matches.[1]

Your results will likely begin with the websites of French restaurants in Manhattan, online reviews of these restaurants, guides to fine dining in the Metro New York area, and so on. The end of your list may well contain the homepage of someone who lives in Batavia, New York, and once ate

French food in Paris, or the Restaurant Association of New City, Illinois, as these represent partial matches of your keywords ("French," "restaurant" and "New City," respectively).

Once you've learned the basics of using e-mail and the web, learning to work search engines is the single most important skill you'll need to effectively use the Internet.[2] The ability to conduct a search and filter out unwanted results will dramatically increase your ability to find what you're looking for on the web and, in turn, make spending time online more enjoyable and productive. One of the great things about the web is that there's literally something on it for everyone; teaching your students effective search methods (or using those methods yourself to build good collections of web links for them) will allow them to find things online that really are there just for them.

There are many good, general-use search engines that you can use for free. None of them is perfect; idiosyncrasies in the way the engines are programmed mean that one might miss one website during a search while another will skip over a different site during the same search. Google (http://www.google.com) is a very popular engine whose technology also powers Yahoo! searches (http://www.yahoo.com). HotBot (http://www.hotbot.com) and Lycos (www.lycos.com) are also good ones to try. An interesting take on searching is Copernic (www.copernic.com), which actually is a meta-engine that automatically runs your search on several different search engines and then compiles and compares the results. The hits that come up near the top of the most engines are returned to you as the top matches for your search.[3]

Whatever search engine or meta-engine you use, bear in mind that just because a web page is returned at the top of your results doesn't necessarily mean it's the best match for your needs. Search engines are getting "smarter" (more intelligently programmed) all the time, but they still rely on cold logic much more than most of us do when selecting keywords to feed into them.

For example, let's say you're looking for a middle-school-level resource on the history of Prospect Park in Brooklyn, New York. You might search for "Prospect Park Brooklyn NY," which certainly seems like a good place to start. The problem is that the results you get back won't be filtered by content difficulty level; you're as likely to get back a Ph.D. dissertation in urban planning or Dutch-American history as you are seventh-grade-level materials on how the park was designed and the influence of public space on the mixing of ethnic cultures in New York City. Similarly, you could wind up with a host of websites discussing the biology and geology of Brooklyn and not its history.

LET THOSE YOU TRUST WORK FOR YOU

So how do we go about searching for education-specific resources on the web? Well, learning to jockey a search engine is a good first step. Even better, though, is discovering some good education-specific search engines and websites to keep in your arsenal of content-finding tools.

Traditional educational publishers and newer education-specific websites offer lots of free content online. Start by looking at the textbooks and other nonelectronic materials you already use in your classes. Who publishes the ones you've come to know and love? Try running a general search for the authors and publishers of books that you already use; a trusted source of information is valuable, and maybe they have a website with new or supplemental material not available in print.

Also, much as the best sources of new information are often friends or colleagues who point you to resources they've come to rely upon, many websites will feature links, pages to guide you to other sites worth a look. So if your favorite author has a website, check to see if there's a link page pointing to additional authors and sources he or she trusts; if an author you like finds them worthwhile, maybe you will, too.

I used to work at bigchalk.com, an educational web company started in the mid-1990s.[4] The core of bigchalk's business was making online resources readily available to K–12 educators, and the heart and soul of their business model was the acquisition of Homework Central. Homework Central was basically a database of website links interfaced to a website (like a search engine); it contained very little in the way of original educational content, resources, or other copyrightable material. Homework Central was also much more than just a database of links. What made Homework Central successful—useful to educators and ultimately attractive to bigchalk.com as an acquisition—was the thought and effort put into selecting and organizing those links.

Homework Central employed two main types of workers: editors and programmers. The editors were experts in their fields of knowledge and they worked at finding the best resources for educators on the web within their subject area. The content division of Homework Central's offices housed a team of graduate students and other intellectual types, many of whom worked part-time combing the web for hours on end in search of, say, the best websites to use when teaching elementary school students about Thomas Jefferson. Editors found their sites and then entered them into a database arranged by subject matter and age group (elementary/middle/high school).

The database that the editors used was developed and maintained by a team of programmers. This division of labor is fairly common in knowledge-driven businesses: editors are responsible for finding or creating the content and programmers make sure that content makes it into the computers, resides there in an orderly fashion, and is correctly formatted for publication. What made Homework Central special was the way in which the editors and programmers interacted from the beginning to make sure the database best showed off the data. Showing off the data, in this case, meant making it as useful as possible for educators and students. They decided to call this marriage of content and technology "The Knowledge."

What's great about The Knowledge is that it quickly points you to what you're looking for *and* suggests places you might want to visit later. The database is designed so that related websites are grouped together but the definitions of "related" and "grouped" are fully employed to take advantage of the nature of the web.

The Knowledge is a commercial form of leveraging word of mouth to your advantage when searching for quality educational resources online. Experts were employed to comb the web, find good content, and organize it in a useful manner. I trusted those experts and liked the way they organized the material, so I used the site and used to recommend it to my friends and colleagues.

There are, of course, hundreds of other websites devoted to cataloging educational resources for your use, and many of them are quite good. It's well worth your time to peruse a few, follow their links, and decide for yourself which will become your favorites to use and recommend to others.[5] This isn't so different from how you recommend a babysitter, book, or bottle of wine to a friend. The Net is geared by design toward a ready exchange of information, passed from person to person. It's so easy to copy a site's address into an e-mail and send it along to a fellow educator, why wouldn't you let them in on your best online resource secrets?

As important as sharing these resources with other educators is sharing them with your students and asking them to share their favorites with you. Even if they're more interested in fantasy baseball statistics than supplemental resources for your Earth science lessons, students will benefit from knowing where to look for information and how to sort out the good from the bad.

A great way to get kids used to using the web for research is to prompt them to find the best, most up-to-date information available on their favorite topic, whatever it is (so long as it's appropriate material for school). Draw the students into the meta-lesson of searching and sifting through information by leveraging the excitement that comes with what they're already interested in. Use that excitement to foster mastery of the skills involved in researching. Students already invested in the worth of the information they're searching for will be more motivated to do the work of learning to use a new research method (in this case, searching the web). Then, when it's time to research a topic of your choosing, students won't be frustrated by learning to use the technology; they can get straight to the business of exploring the information itself.

FROM SEARCHING TO BUILDING: COMMUNICATING ONLINE

In the previous chapter I mentioned that one of my favorite things about the web is how easy it is to see how web pages are built using the "View Source" command. Learning HTML isn't for everyone, nor does everyone need to know how to hand-code a web page from scratch. But it's a good idea for anyone who uses the Net often to have at least a familiarity with how to build a web page.

The web has become so popular because it's a convenient way to access information. If you're mastering the fine art of searching and sifting through web pages to gather the best information pertinent to your teaching and learning, why not develop the skills to share your findings with colleagues? And if your students have found the *best* places online to find out the latest gossip on their favorite television stars—or rather, supplement their study of Thomas Jefferson—shouldn't they also have the tools to share those resources with their friends?

There are a number of commercially available software programs that let you construct websites without your having to know a single line of HTML code. These programs are known as "WYSIWYG" editors because they're based on the notion that What You See Is What You Get. Basically, you use a graphical interface to select a color scheme for the page, lay out and format text, and add images and other media to the mix. When you're done arranging things, the program automatically generates the HTML code that will render your page in a web browser.

Lots of coders (and wannabe coders like myself) didn't trust the first generations of WYSIWYGs to generate "clean code." But advances in the editors and standardization of the HTML itself has made today's batch of WYSIWYGs quite handy and reliable for easy generation of even complex web pages. Macromedia's *Dreamweavel* has matured into a powerful and popular WYSIWYG web-authoring tool.

Education is all about understanding, and any student learning to create web pages should have at least a cursory understanding of the code that generates the magic behind the scenes. Practically speaking, knowing basic HTML makes it much easier to create and edit pages, especially when you don't have your WYSIWYG to lean on. Plus, a student who knows the basics of what's going on in HTML code can use View Source to explore the inner workings of more sophisticated web pages, perhaps sparking a lifelong interest in computer science.

Here, then, is a simple but practical lesson plan you can use to teach your students (and yourself) to understand basic HTML and hand-code your own web pages.

Lesson #2: Building Web Pages with HTML

Objective: To familiarize students with the basics of HTML, the code used to program web pages. In this lesson, students will learn simple HTML commands and use them to construct a web page suitable for publishing on the World Wide Web. Students will gain some understanding of and appreciation for what makes the web work. Students interested in learning more about HTML can use this basic knowledge as a starting point for further explorations using online tutorials.

Age Level: Sixth grade through adult
Skill Level: Beginner/Intermediate
Time Required: 25–45 minutes
Materials Needed: Computers running Mac OS or Windows with text editing and web browsing software (which should come preinstalled).

Note: This lesson plan has been written for Mac OS X but can be adapted for whatever edition of the Mac or Windows operating system you are using. HTML is designed to work on multiple platforms. The web browser used here is Internet Explorer, but any current web browser will yield the same results. In Windows, the Mac application "Finder" is the basic application screen without documents or files selected, an "alias" is referred to as a "shortcut," and the application "Text Edit" is "Notepad."

1. Prepare the computers so that each one has aliases (shortcuts) to "Text Edit" and "Internet Explorer" on the desktop.
2. Assign one computer to each student or group of students. This lesson is based on hands-on usage of the system and so works best with no more than two students to a computer.
3. Using the blackboard or a handout, go over the basic structure of an HTML page. Explain the following elements of HTML code:
   a) Tags are used to designate the beginning and end of a command or section of the page. Tags always appear in <brackets> and generally come in pairs, with one half opening a tag and the other half closing it. Examples of tags are <HTML> and </HTML> (marking the beginning and end of an HTML page), <HEAD> and </HEAD> (marking the beginning and end of the header section of a page), and <a> and </a> (marking the beginning and end of a hyperlink). Tags may be written using upper or lowercase characters.
   b) The HTML, head, and body sections. As explained above, the HTML tags always come at the beginning and end of a page. The head and body sections of a page separate header information from the main body of the web page. Header information can include the title of a page and other information used to define and describe the page. The body is where the text, images, and other usable elements of a page are coded. Remember that all three of these elements are designated with pairs of tags like this:

```
<HTML>
<Head>
This is the header
</Head>
<Body>
And this is the body
</Body>
</HTML>
```

   c) Formatting, Image, and Media Tags. Tags are used in the body of an HTML page to describe what will appear on the page and how it will look and function. Formatting tags are used to change the size, style, and color of text. Examples of formatting tags are <Bold>**Bold Text**</Bold>, <I>*Italicized Text*</I>, and <H3> Headline Text</H3> if not (headlines come in different sizes, designated by numbers). The <br> tag is used to designate a line break (carriage return) and is one of the few tags that are not used in pairs. Image and media tags are used to embed various bits of photos, graphics, and multimedia in the page.

4. Explain to students that you are going to create web pages to keep track of your favorite places on the web. Students will be able to use their web browsers to get the exact names and addresses of their favorite sites to use in the project.

5. Have students launch the application Text Edit. They will then have a blank file to start with.

6. Have students start their web pages with the following code, which begins the page and creates a header section, including a title:

```
<HTML>
<HEAD>
<TITLE>My Favorite Places on the Web</TITLE>
</HEAD>
</HTML>
```

   Explain that they have actually just created a working web page with a title that will show up in the title bar of the browser window. Have the students save their work by choosing File ➜ Save from the menu bar and entering "places.html" as the name of the file. Explain that the names of HTML files always have to end with ".html" in order to work.[6]

7. A web page with a title but no content isn't very useful, so now you will create the body section of the web page. This is where students will list their favorite places on the web, including descriptions and working hyperlinks. Get them started with a useful link—a search engine. I have chosen Google for my search link, and this is what the HTML now looks like:

```
<HTML>
<HEAD>
<TITLE>My Favorite Places on the Web</TITLE>
</HEAD>
<BODY>
<H3>My List of Favorite Places</H3>
Google is a great search engine for finding anything you want online.
<a href="http://www.google.com">Click here</a> to get to
www.google.com.<br>
</BODY>
</HTML>
```

Have all of your students enter the same code into their pages and save their work. Explain what is going on here: The <BODY> tag starts the body of the page, which is what users will see. The <H3> tags make the text "My List of Favorite Places" show up as a headline in big, bold text, followed by an automatic line break. The next line is a description of Google, which will show up as plain text. The <a href> tag begins a hyperlink. So in this case the text "Click here" will show up as a hyperlink to the web address entered into the tag. The </a> tag closes the hyperlink, so the words that follow ("to get to …") are back to normal text. The <br> tag adds a line break. Finally, the </BODY> tag closes the body of the page.

8. Emphasize how important it is to be precise when writing HTML code. The computer will not understand spelling mistakes and other typos, so students should double-check their work.

9. Have students use Internet Explorer to look at their web pages. They should launch Internet Explorer and then use the File → Open command from the menu bar to find their "places.html" file and open it. The web page should appear in the browser with a title on top and a headline and description/link to Google in the main window. If there are errors, or if nothing shows up at all, double-check the HTML code. Beginners (and experts!) often forget to close a tag or they make small

typos that cause problems. Don't panic if this happens—just double check for typographical errors.

10. Students should then go back to Text Edit and add more favorite places to their lists. To do this, they'll need to know the exact web addresses (URLs) of their places. Then, all they have to do is copy the HTML used for the Google entry and change the description and link address. For example, here is my code with a second entry added for Threebase.com, my personal web page:

```
<HTML>
<HEAD>
<TITLE>My Favorite Places on the Web</TITLE>
</HEAD>
<BODY>
<H3>My List of Favorite Places</H3>
Google is a great search engine for finding anything you want online.
<a href="http://www.google.com">Click here</a> to get to
www.google.com.<br>
Threebase.com is my website, with links to my writing and music.
<a href="http://www.threebase.com">Click here</a> to visit Three
base.<br>
</BODY>
</HTML>
```

The description you write doesn't affect the hyperlink itself. The link is determined by the <a href="..."> tag. Whatever is inside those quotation marks is the address that the browser will jump to when the link is clicked. Make sure to use the proper notation, including "http://" when coding your links. Advanced students may point out that you can also link directly to e-mail addresses and audiovisual files using this method.

11. Repeat step 10 until students' lists are complete. After adding each new entry, students should save their work and then use the "Refresh" command in Internet Explorer to make sure that their page has been successfully updated. Note that changes made to HTML code won't actually show up on a web page unless (1) the HTML page has been saved, and (2) the page has been reopened or refreshed in the web browser.

12. At the end of this lesson your students should have basic web pages that will work in browsers. If you are familiar with more

formatting tags you can show students how to change the font face, size, and color of their text, how to set the background color of their page, and so on.[7] Also, if you know how to do so, you can upload these pages to a school web server for viewing online. Make sure to give each file a unique name if you choose to post them to the web.

At this point it's okay if students don't understand the nuances or conceptual underpinning of things like the <a href> tag. The goal is to have them go through the process of building a web page to familiarize themselves with the notion that creating a web page takes work; it's not magic, and it's not impossible. Any of them—and any of you—can learn to create and post your own web pages. This is what makes the web so revolutionary: for the first time in our history, the cost of mass-publishing information is affordable to individuals and not just large organizations/corporations. Sure, America Online can afford to spend more time and money to create fancy graphics and sophisticated multimedia than your school can—but in theory, and even in practice, you can reach just as many people with your message as they do with theirs.

THE IMPACT OF TECHNOLOGY ON FREE SPEECH

A good corollary to this lesson for older students is to discuss the wider impact of the masses having access to such a powerful means of broadcasting information. Much has been made recently of the role of the Internet in propagating hate speech, giving would-be criminals easy access to nefarious documents like bomb-building plans, and allowing extremist organizations to organize and spread their messages over long distances with great ease. Just as we wouldn't blame the paper and ink itself for the penning of a hate manifesto, we can't blame the computers and telephone wires for these uses of the Internet.

Discuss with your students how the Internet can be used to disseminate ideas and how those ideas may or may not be protected in the United States and abroad by free speech laws. Should free speech laws be amended when it comes to the Internet? What about television and radio?

What about when it comes to giving minors access to these mediums—should the laws be amended to specifically protect children? Is there a difference between exposing children to violent content online and exposing them to violence in movies and video games?

The Chinese government has allowed the Internet within its borders, but citizens' access to approximately one in ten websites is blocked for reasons stemming from political ideology.[8] Should the U.S. government adopt a similar stance when it comes to websites promoting hate and destruction? How does the Constitution apply to this debate?

Technology and law is fast becoming a critical area of debate and policymaking in the United States. Since 1990, dozens of important and hotly contested bills relating to the Internet and digital technologies have been introduced to local, state, and federal governing bodies in attempts to write the laws of cyberspace. The wide range of topics addressed in these bills speaks to the increasing pervasiveness of computing in everyday life and the ways in which technology is changing the landscape of our culture and workplaces.

Everything from the legality of linking to someone's website without their permission to deciding whether online commerce should be taxed to the right of your government and employer to keep tabs on your e-mail and web surfing activities is up for debate. Cyberspace truly is the next frontier; since the Internet is a global network that transcends international boundaries, should an international governing body be established to regulate it? These are but a few of the questions to be debated, answered, and debated again as computer-mediated communications further blur the lines between public and private space and the political borders that separate states and countries around the world.

WILL THE INTERNET FIT ON THAT DESK?

A friend of mine likes to tell the story of the time he went shopping for a desk. He was at a furniture store looking one over when a woman walked up to him and asked for some advice. "My husband needs a desk and I think he'd like this one," she explained. "But he uses the computer a lot and I don't know if it's big enough. Will the Internet fit on this desk?"

The answer, of course, is "Yes and No." The Internet, as we've already established, is a giant network of computers that crisscrosses the globe connected by antennas, fiber optic cables, and the like. So, no, it couldn't possibly fit on even the largest of desks. However, to access the Net all you need is a computer with the ability to talk to other computers—one that can "get online." Computers like this can not only fit on even the smallest of schoolhouse desks but some of them will fit in the palm of your hand.

Not fifty years ago most computers in the United States took up entire rooms, cost tens of thousands of dollars to build, and were accessible only to elite academics, businessmen, and scientists. These early computing machines had no keyboards or monitors but relied upon punch cards (think of a cross between a bingo card and the ticket you receive when driving on a toll road) for input and output. Data was fed into the computer using a card punched according to a coded system, and the computer would run a program on that data and return a freshly punched card. The operator or programmer would then decode this new card to get the results of the program.

Everyone involved in the process, from the designers of the computer to the programmers and operators of the machine, was highly trained and working in special laboratories or computer rooms sequestered from the rest of their business or university. Maybe the computer scientists didn't all wear white lab coats while they worked, but it does make for a nice image that's probably not so far from the truth.

How far we've come in fifty years! In the midst of working on this book, my laptop broke. I called Apple Computer and within two days they sent me a padded box for shipping the machine to their repair center halfway across the country. Two days after that I had my laptop back with half of its innards replaced and working as good as new. At one to two thousand dollars for a new model, it's still more economical to fix a computer than replace it when it breaks, but before long it may not be. Somewhere in my apartment there are several old Macs that once cost over a thousand dollars each, and now, though they're still fully functional, don't get much use because they can't do most of the things my two-year-old laptop can.

My friend Glen took a different tack when his cell phone was stolen recently. Glen's phone was fairly sophisticated, with the abilities to send and receive e-mail and play games in addition to the usual phone capabilities. Buying a replacement would have cost him about $150. However, a service provider in his area was offering a special deal on a new phone they'd just introduced to the marketplace. What he got represents both the cutting edge of today's technology and a mere peek into what's in store for our technological tomorrow.

Glen's new phone, the Danger Hiptop, is a little bit longer and thicker than a man's wallet. It fits in the palm of his hand and, though heavier than most cell phones, it's largely forgotten when clipped to his belt. There are buttons and a thumb wheel on the front, along with a speaker and microphone for making telephone calls, and a gray-scale screen that measures about two inches diagonally. The screen can be twisted open to reveal a full QWERTY keyboard underneath that is meant to be typed on with your thumbs. There is also a headset jack to allow for privacy in speaking and listening, and an expansion jack designed with an eye toward the future. Currently there is only one expansion device available: a snap-on camera that comes with the unit and takes low-resolution color photos.[9]

Glen lives in the San Francisco, California, area and so most of the time he is within service range for his phone. This means that virtually wherever he goes, whenever he wants, he can place or receive a phone call to or from anywhere in the world. He can also send/receive short text messages with other cell-phone users, send/receive e-mail, and take color photos and attach them to e-mails. He can also browse the web—the phone has a standard HTML browser that can access most web pages and also run interactive JAVA applets—and chat with people via instant messenger service. And he can play games. All without a desk, without wires, and clipped to his belt wherever he goes.

Glen's phone is not the most sophisticated or expensive of its kind. This particular model was developed and marketed specifically for the teenage and young adult markets. It's cute and colorful and hip from the inside out. Similar devices meant for businesspeople sport different designs and slightly different features but do basically the same thing: provide access to communications and information without regard to the physical limitations imposed by desks, phone lines, and office buildings.

Advertising campaigns in support of these gadgets tout this disregard for physical location when it comes to increasing productivity and the ability to communicate. A man dressed in a suit and carrying a briefcase is pictured sitting in an airport terminal. Beneath the photo is a caption: "15 minutes. Wait or communicate?"

ALWAYS ON: THE PORTABLE, PERVASIVE INTERNET

"Moore's law" is used to describe the growth of computing power by measuring our ability to fit more and more transistors onto a microchip over time. The law, named for Gordon Moore, founder of Intel Corporation, states that the transistor-to-chip ratio will double every eighteen to twenty-four months. Relative computing power available to users at a given price will grow at the same rate. In other words, a thousand dollars today will get you a computer twice as powerful as the one you just bought a year and a half ago.

Ray Kurzweil, in his book *The Age of Spiritual Machines*, predicts the death of Moore's law by the year 2020, citing a number of advanced computing technologies already waiting in the wings to take the place of transistor-based microchips. Kurzweil's book is a forward-thinking, insightful read full of bold predictions about our technology-laden future, but even he may have underestimated the rapid rate of change where computers are concerned. Moore's law may well expire sometime closer to 2010 than 2020. Before that happens, though, new methods of building chips—such as moving from flat to three-dimensional designs—could leapfrog the pace of Moore's law.[10]

Assuming that Moore's law holds on for just a little longer, what can we expect from personal computing in just the next five to ten years? We've moved from room-filling mainframe computers to pocket-sized, web-browsing cell phones in fifty years, so what could possibly be next? And what effects might new computing devices and technologies have on the ways we teach and learn?

First of all, expect the widespread adoption of handheld, wireless Net devices in America by 2005. Glen already has his, and soon you'll have yours as well. Much as cell phones changed from expensive toys for the rich and famous to readily available consumer goods in the span of a few years, so too will this new breed of Star Trek–like communicators migrate to the mainstream.

Those of us who want it will soon have constant access to telephone calls, e-mail, web browsing, instant messaging, and personal information management (PIM) such as calendars and contact organizers—anytime, anywhere. As the price of hardware like miniature color displays and tiny, powerful processor chips drops, the cost of these gadgets will become minimal. Just as cellular service providers have begun to offer free phones with new service contracts, so too will these web gadgets be free of charge to users who sign contracts for paid Net access.

What your money gets you will increase dramatically, also. As the availability of wireless bandwidth increases, more and more data will be sent between users at faster speeds. That is to say that just as DSL and cable modems have started to bring high-speed Net access to home users, similar technologies will become available to wireless carriers and their customers.

High-speed wireless networks won't help you speak more quickly, but they will let you send and receive more data with your phone. Color web pages with animations, e-mail, and picture messaging, even audio and video—all of this and more coming soon to your hip pocket. While this may sound like something straight out of a science fiction movie, the fact is that our friends overseas in Europe and Asia are already watching videos on their mobile phones. Although the quality may not yet be on a par with your local movie theater, the technology is there and it's being used.[11]

Another technology to be on the lookout for over the next few years is "convergence." Convergence is really more of a concept or trend than a technology, and it's one of those ideas that turned into an ugly buzzword before its time. Way back in the Golden Age of the Dot Com (circa 1999), the word *convergence* was thrown around at certain conferences and cocktail parties to describe how the Internet was going to make many things possible and create much new wealth.

Unfortunately, many of the people using the term ultimately proved themselves more interested in the getting rich than in making things possible, and so convergence remained more of a vague marketing promise than a plausible method of combining, say, the best features of television viewing and web browsing. If you'll recall, during those days the surge of the stock market was built on such promises.

The idea of convergence that you'll see over the next few years actually isn't that much different from what those folks were talking about over cocktails in 1999. Computing technology has been embedded in "noncomputer" goods for some time now. Your car probably has several computer chips that help with everything from monitoring the braking system to remembering your favorite radio stations. Modern heating and cooling systems are run by computerized thermostats, and microwave ovens rely on computers to keep track of time and temperature. Computers really have been creeping further and further into daily life since their invention.

Convergence isn't just about using computing technology away from the PC, though. Convergence in this sense refers to the use of telecommunications to enhance a consumer product or technology. Basically, we're talking about Internet-ready appliances, interactive television, and using that pocket-sized web device to program the VCR in your house before you leave school or the workplace at the end of the day.[12]

When I was a senior in high school in 1991, people didn't have computer networks in their homes. We barely had one at my high school, and it was primarily used to access our library's card catalog. Today it's relatively cheap and effortless to network PCs together in your home. It's easy to connect them without wires and even to most of the other PCs in the world via the Internet. Things have changed quickly. What will happen next is that the other devices in your home will start to come online, too.

The July 2003 issue of *Wired* magazine features an article about the future of home entertainment as relates to digital media and copyright laws. The article begins with a description of the "Microsoft Home," a house in Redmond, Washington, that the giant software corporation uses to model the future for business partners and the media:

> Your future home may seem familiar at first. You still dig stainless steel appliances, exposed beams, blond hardwood floors, halogen track lighting, and rice-paper shades. But beyond the aesthetics, everything has changed. The lights and heat automatically fine-tune to your preference the moment you cross the threshold. A screen on the wall in the foyer reads your email aloud as you hang your coat. Your kitchen has become your own private sous chef. Run a chicken pot pie beneath the barcode reader on the microwave and it sets the time and temperature. Break out the food processor

and some baking material; your home recognizes RFID tags in the bag of flour and offers to help. "How about focaccia?" you suggest. The lights dim, and a recipe shines down from above on your black Corian countertop as the oven begins to preheat.

And digital media is everywhere. "Suspicious Minds" greets you in full-home surround sound. The family's collective music library is accessible from any room, on every device. You can cue up a movie on a kitchen monitor while cooking and finish it on the plasma in the den—or the projection screen in the media room. A central media server supplies entertainment throughout, seamlessly streaming content wherever there is demand.[13]

Our future homes will be full of networked devices, scanners and sensors, and televisions and microwave ovens all connected to each other via central computers that will predict for us what we want them to do. Ten or twenty years from now, the idea of sitting down in front of a computer screen to "go online" will be nothing more than a quaint bit of nostalgia. *Everything* in our lives will be online by then.

INTELLIGENT DEVICES AND EDUCATION

While the notion of a convergence between the vast knowledge of the Internet and rapidly improving consumer electronics technology sounds great for making home life better, what good can it do for teaching and learning? What could an Internet-ready toaster possibly have to do with teaching someone to read?

Well, not much really. But a Net-ready electronic textbook could do a lot for the cause. Consumer electronics companies generate a lot of revenue and so they have a lot of money to spend on new product research and development, hence the constant stream of electronic gadgets that proliferate in our collective consciousness and flood our television commercials. Educational technology may not be quite the big business that televisions and microwave ovens are, but some serious time, effort, and yes, money are being spent on leveraging all of this increased bandwidth and processing power for the sake of teaching and learning.

From math games that run on your computer to picture books that talk to your children, educational technology products strive to make learning adaptive and personalized, customized, and self-maintained. While a computer (or even a talking picture book) can never take the place of a real-live teacher, the ed-tech products now starting to appear in our schools and stores do promise personalized attention for learners in a world where high student-to-teacher ratios are too often the norm.

In the past twenty years, school computer labs have progressed from running the LOGO programming language and the "Lemonade Game" on monochrome green screens to running interactive CD-ROMs that teach science students about the human body with full-color, digital video footage shot by tiny robot-controlled cameras that are helping to unlock mysteries of life once thought forever out of our reach. Actually, some schools now use LOGO-based programs that allow students to program robots that roam around the classroom. That's quite a ways from the on-screen "turtle" that I remember.[14]

The computer has become a multimedia tool suitable for production and presentation of very sophisticated, engrossing educational materials spanning all subject matter and age levels. The videocassette recorder made widespread dissemination of moving pictures possible in the 1970s and '80s. In the 1990s, the proliferation of low-cost, high-capacity storage media like CD- and DVD-ROMs brought those moving pictures to the in-teractive environment of the computer screen. For the educator, the dif-ference between the two was the difference between an entire class gath-ered en masse around a single screen and small groups or individuals in front of their own screens, with keyboard controls to allow for self-paced watching and rewatching of the material, and access to supplementary materials on demand.

The convergence of interactive media with the on-demand information flow afforded by the Internet takes the latter scenario—students working through material on an individually controlled, self-paced basis—and adds to it the ability for the material itself to be expanded and updated on a near-constant basis. Textbooks can be printed with URLs of online re-sources included for supplementary or updated information. The text-books themselves can be delivered in electronic format to eliminate the need for printing updated versions; rather than buying a fleet of new hard-bound books whenever a new edition is published, educators can sub-scribe to a volume and have updates delivered to them through the Net. Students, of course, will need a computer of some sort (laptop, e-book,

PDA) to read the text, but the text can theoretically remain constantly updated at dramatically reduced publishing costs—not to mention the positive impact that paperless texts can have on the environment.

A traditional math textbook contains practice questions and answers to help students achieve mastery. Often, some of these Q&As are supplemented with full explanations of how the solution is obtained, but cost and space constraints make thoroughly explaining each and every question impossible. Now imagine an electronic version of a math textbook, perhaps one that a student can download to a handheld e-book device. This electronic book has a screen for viewing, a speaker and headphone jack for listening, and modest input capabilities (a few buttons, maybe a touch screen and pen stylus). To keep costs down, it's not nearly as sophisticated as a full-fledged laptop computer, but it can store a semester or two's worth of textbooks.

A device like this would allow publishers to include thorough explanations for *all* of the math problems in their textbooks without worrying about the physical size of the books. The problems could also be made interactive—students could solve the problems and get instant feedback on their work from the software itself or even from a tutor via live video-conferencing. Additionally, the problem of learning styles could be addressed with supplementary materials—visual learners could opt for supplementary graphics, animations, and charts to help explain the material, aural learners could listen to the text being read to them as they follow along onscreen, and so on.

Now imagine this portable e-book connected to the Internet. Supplementary math problems would be available on demand to students who needed them. The problems could be customized to different subject areas and skill levels (a feature commonly known as "adaptive learning") and automatically downloaded as needed by "intelligent texts." For example, a student who did well on a set of multiplication problems but struggled with division would automatically get an extra set of division problems at the end of the chapter. Students who excelled with the material would get a set of advanced problems—or even self-paced learning units presenting new material—to keep them challenged and engaged.

Problem sets could be downloaded from the publisher or custom-created by educators for their classes. The enormity of free content already available on the web could be tapped into to further supplement the material.

Student work could be automatically collected by the teacher via e-mail, assessed electronically, and returned with comments via e-mail.

The possibilities begin to mount rather quickly, and this is just within the framework of mimicking the print texts we are used to. The fun begins when we allow ourselves to think outside of the box, as they say, and abandon our notions of what educational materials have always been, in favor of what they could be.[15]

MAINTAINING A BALANCE

The potential that lies within a new generation of Internet-connected devices is enormous and exciting for educators. At the core of thinking about how best to make use of all of this technology, though, must also be serious thinking about when *not* to use it. For all of the good there is to be had from enhancing teaching and learning with technology, there is a danger of overdoing it as well. The danger in deploying educational technology should be familiar to anyone who likes to watch television, eat dessert, or lie out on the beach on a sunny August day. Overdoing it, no matter what the activity, is never good for you.

As a musician, one of the most important lessons I was taught—and still work to master—is knowing when *not* to play. The impact of a great melody or rhythm can be made more powerful by figuring out exactly what makes it sound so good and leaving everything else out. Similarly, a great song can easily be ruined by overplaying. Even if the overplaying comes from the heart and is done with great skill, more often than not, less really is more.

Computers are exciting because they're always full of surprises. New software, innovations in hardware and design, even new tricks you didn't know your old PC could perform—there's always something innovative awaiting us when it comes to technology. Students really like this aspect of working with computers: it's exciting to see something magical and new happen right before your eyes, and even better when you learn how to make it happen yourself. Computers may not be for everyone, but as anyone who's ever wasted an evening surfing the Net knows, it's dangerously easy to spend more time online than you mean to, getting yourself sucked deeper and deeper into the screen until you've lost all track of the physical world.[16]

For all the joy I feel as a teacher when students of mine are turned on to learning about computers, I also feel it my duty to help them become well-rounded people. I'm more than happy to give a student extra help or show him advanced concepts during a free period, but I also feel compelled to chase him out of the computer lab if I think he is overdoing it, particularly when it comes to eleven-year-olds struggling with the social anxieties of early adolescence. Coming in a few lunch periods in a row to work on a project is one thing; spending every lunch period all semester in front of the screen by yourself while your peers are getting to know one another in the cafeteria and on the playground is quite another.

The lure and dangers of spending too much time on the computer are easy to see in the delicate social world of junior high school, but they extend well into the adult world, too. Like a good book, movie, or piece of music, the computer can provide an escape from the dealings and pressures of the social world. Working on a program, designing a web page, or playing a game can be an engrossing experience that challenges the mind and captivates the imagination without worries about how your peers perceive you.

The computer provides feedback without judgment, or at least its judgments are based on programming logic and not on more subjective emotions and opinions. When you're nine, just beginning to discover who you are and what you value, and faced with the harsh reality that those things don't match up with whatever's trendy and cool in your school during a given week, life can be pretty hard—not to mention confusing. The computer, with its consistent rules and capacity to provide instant feedback, can prove quite a draw.

Add to that the unique social environment that the Internet provides through e-mail, instant messaging, chat rooms, and bulletin boards. When you're online, how tall you are or how clear your skin is doesn't matter. Nobody can see if your arms are skinny or muscled, or if your clothes are fashionable or out of style. All they can see is what you want them to see: your thoughts, words, art, and ideas are yours to display or keep under wraps as you wish and how you wish.

Whether you're into radio-controlled cars or gothic art, heavy metal or chamber music, there are other people out there who share your interests, and the Internet makes it easier to find them. You can read their words, find their e-mail addresses, and interact with them in chat rooms. This is a wonderful resource for the isolated, and a powerful draw for the lonely.

As an educator taking on the task of constructively using the Internet with your students, it is your job to introduce them to this resource and to teach them to manage it. You may not be showing your students where to find chat rooms, but if you teach them to use the Internet to research topics they're interested in, sooner or later they will discover the many chat rooms in which people are already talking about those subjects.

Much is made of the need to protect our children from inappropriate content available online. While it is important to do what we can to keep adult content away from the eyes and ears of children who aren't yet ready for it, it's just as important to make sure that we are aware of what effect all of that time behind the screen is having on them.

The Internet is a wonderful resource with much to lend to teaching and learning alike. It can help bring people together, fostering communication and opening pathways to understanding between diverse peoples for whom no common ground had previously existed. Let's not forget, however, that the most we can expect from technology is to mediate our interactions. It is still up to us to decide how best to make use of and regulate these new opportunities for interaction. While technology can be a wonderful thing, it is the people who make and use it that matter most of all.

NOTES

1. While all search engines rank results according to how many of a query's keywords were found in various sites' content, the different engines use different methods to sort within those rankings. Google, for instance, looks at how many other pages *link to* a particular page. So of two pages returned containing all of your query's keywords, the one that has the most other sites pointing to it will be listed first on your results page. This populist method is in keeping with the word-of-mouth spirit of the web and has proven quite effective and popular.

2. The basics of using the web include being able to access specific web pages by entering their URLs, jump from page to page using hyperlinks, and use the browser's navigational and menu commands to open and close windows, download files, and go back to revisit pages in your session history. These skills can be learned using the basic techniques of menu exploration as described in chapter two. Alternatively, good tutorials are available online at the websites at the end of this chapter.

3. Other popular search engines on the World Wide Web include Altavista (http://www.altavista.com) and Ask Jeeves (http://www.ask.com). Good search

engines for kids include Yahooligans! (http://www.yahooligans.com) and Ask Jeeves for Kids (http://www.ajkids.com).

4. Bigchalk.com was formed as the web-specific corporate child of Infonautics and ProQuest. In mid-2000, as the dot-coms started to lose favor on Wall Street, bigchalk.com shortened its name to bigchalk. Then, in early 2003, the company was acquired by ProQuest, which has changed the business strategy again. As of press time, bigchalk.com was still up and running, but its services were no longer free of charge to users. Homework Central is no longer available on bigchalk.com as the result of business decisions made by bigchalk and explained in further detail at http://www.bigchalk.com/cgi-bin/WebObjects/WOPortal.woa/db/about-us/change_notice.html.

5. For a few starting points, see the list of educational web resources in the following suggested reading section.

6. Actually, this is not a hard and fast rule. Today's web pages can end with variants on the .html file extension including ".htm," ".shtml," and others. Pages generated on the fly by database-driven sites often end with an extension pertaining to the kind of database being run, such as ".asp" (active server page), ".jsp" (java servlet page), or ".php" (an open-source system gaining in popularity for its cost-effectiveness and ease of use). For our purposes here, it is wisest to instruct students to name their HTML pages with the .html extension.

7. Several web pages provide quick reference to HTML tags and other web programming essentials. See the suggested reading list.

8. http://news.bbc.co.uk/1/hi/world/asia-pacific/2541431.stm

9. Danger introduced a second edition of the Hiptop with a color screen and other new features in the summer of 2003; http://www.danger.com

10. Ray Kurzweil, *The Age of Spiritual Machines* (New York: Penguin Books, 1999), 21.

11. A large part of what is keeping the United States from being in the forefront of adopting new technologies such as "third generation" (3G) wireless phones is not our inability to produce the technology but rather the size and structure of our marketplace. Whereas many technologically advanced nations are ruled by governments that mandate companies to adopt one standard or another of new technologies, America maintains a relatively unregulated free-market economy. As such, competing versions of similar technologies are simultaneously introduced to the marketplace and it is often consumer preference that dictates which brands and versions last and which wither on the vine. While this promotes competition and what you might call healthy capitalism, it also can serve to stand in the way of the adoption of superior technologies. A good case in point was the battle between VHS and Beta videotape formats in the 1980s. While Beta was far and away the superior technology, consumer preference eventually made VHS a

success while Beta died out. Marketing, politics, and other factors played into the ways in which the two formats were presented to the public, but ultimately it was consumer preference that made VHS the standard for home VCRs.

12. The VCR is soon to be outdated, actually, by its digital counterpart, the digital video recorder (DVR). Also known as a personal video recorder (PVR), DVRs capture video as digital content and store it on DVDs or massive hard drives like those found in PCs. DVRs can be connected to home networks for sharing television programs and digital music between TVs, stereos, and PCs within a house. They also can be connected to the Internet to receive programming information from service providers and also allow users to remotely program recording schedules over the web.

13. Jeffery M. O'Brien, "Bill Gates, Entertainment God," *Wired* (July 2003): 121 and http://www.wired.com/wired/archive/11.07/40gates.html

14. LOGO is a programming language very well suited to teaching that is popular with elementary and junior high school teachers and students. Early versions of LOGO environments featured an onscreen "turtle" who could be made to draw shapes and carry out other tasks with simple, sentence-like programming commands. New products from Lego and other developers allow users to program robots using LOGO. See the suggested links for more information.

15. For a wonderfully inventive take on the possibilities of intelligent texts, and a great read at that, I wholeheartedly recommend Neal Stephenson's cyberpunk novel *The Diamond Age* (see citation under suggested readings).

16. The impact of computers and technology-mediated communication on human behavior is a relatively new and very important field of study. Sherry Turkle is a prominent researcher in the field and an accessible writer. See below for suggested reading.

SUGGESTED READING

Ray Kurzweil, *The Age of Spiritual Machines* (New York: Viking, 1999).

Tammy M. McGraw and John D. Ross, *Distance-Based and Distributed Learning: A Decision Tool for Educational Leaders* (Lanham, Md.: ScarecrowEducation, 2000).

Shawn Morris, *Teaching and Learning Online: A Step-by-Step Guide for Designing an Online K-12 School Program* (Lanham, Md.: ScarecrowEducation, 2002).

Neal Stephenson, *The Diamond Age: Or, Young Lady's Illustrated Primer* (New York: Bantam, 1995).

Sherry Turkle, *Life on the Screen* (New York: Simon & Schuster, 1995).

——. *The Second Self: Computers and the Human Spirit* (New York: Simon & Schuster, 1984).

SUGGESTED LINKS

Educational Resources Online

Andrew Smith's Home Page
   http://www.neosoft.com/neosoft/staff/andrew/default.html
The Children's Literature Web Guide
   http://www.ucalgary.ca/~dkbrown
Classroom Connect
   http://www.classroom.net
Education Index
   http://www.educationindex.com
Education World
   http://www.education-world.com
ENC Online
   http://www.enc.org
HTML Reference
University of Kansas HTML Quick Reference
   http://www.ku.edu/~acs/docs/other/HTML_quick.shtml
W3C HTML Homepage
   http://www.w3.org/MarkUp/
WDG Reference Section
   http://www.htmlhelp.com/reference/

LOGO

LEGO Mindstorms Homepage
   http://mindstorms.lego.com/eng/default.asp
Microworlds Educational Software
   http://www.microworlds.com
MIT Logo Foundation
   http://el.media.mit.edu/logo-foundation/
MIT Logo Foundation Robotics
   http://el.media.mit.edu/logo-foundation/products/robotics.html

Technology and the Future

Dynamism — Next Generation Japanese Electronics
http://www.dynamism.com
Gizmodo Gadget Blog
http:// www.gizmodo.com
Kuro5hin Online Technology News
http://www.kuro5hin.org
PowerBook Central Technology News
http://www.powerbookcentral.com
Slashdot Online Technology News
http://www.slashdot.org
Wired Magazine Homepage
http://www.wired.com

Web-Surfing Tutorials

Centerspan Web-Surfing Tutorial
http://www.centerspan.org/tutorial/surf.htm
Education World Surfing Techniques
http://www.educationworld.com/a_tech/tech078.shtml
Georgetown University Web-Surfing Tutorial
http://www.georgetown.edu/crossroads/workshop1.html

Chapter Four

Ubiquitous Tools: Leveraging Technology Where You Teach

BANK STREET WRITER

Nestled into a side street a few blocks south of Columbia University on Manhattan's Upper West Side, Bank Street College has been in the business of teaching teachers to teach since 1916.[1] Sharing a tall, libraryesque building with the Bank Street School for Children (a progressive, private elementary school that ranks among New York City's best), the college is a decidedly child-centered, school-reform–minded institution dedicated to the thoughtful preparation of new teachers and the continual growth and development of its own faculty. Bank Street hangs its hat on philosophies of equality and humanity in the classroom, an increasingly difficult task for a college whose student teachers, in-service teachers, and graduates venture out into one of the nation's most overcrowded and resource-strapped public school systems.

Bank Street's relationship to technology in the classroom is an interesting one. Years ago, a research effort at the college produced one of the world's first pieces of educational software, "Bank Street Writer." A word processor designed specifically for children, the Bank Street Writer name surely rings bells for those of you who grew up with an Apple IIe in your elementary school classrooms.

Another Bank Street initiative resulted in the 1981 formation of the Center for Children and Technology (CCT), a research and development/consultancy organization devoted to the investigation of the impact of technology in supporting teaching and learning within the context of school reform. Clearly, Bank Street has been on the forefront of progressive development of educational technology since the beginning of the brief history of computers in schools.

Bank Street is also, in the year 2003, a college whose director of instructional technology makes a compelling argument that one of the most important pieces of technology available to students and teachers is available for ninety-nine cents at your local drugstore.

"A yellow highlighter is technology," he said. "It lets you see."

Dr. Marvin Cohen is representative of the missing link between multimillion-dollar outpourings of federal and state funds to purchase computers for schools and the effective use of all that fancy gadgetry once it's delivered to your child's grammar school by the UPS guy. As an educator and knowledgeable technologist who understands that the latest gadgets the technology industry has to sell are often not very useful tools for teachers, Cohen reminds us that the future of educational technology is a sound platform upon which to *begin* our exploration of best practices. "We need to use technology to do things we couldn't do before, and not just to do old things better."

SIMPLE IS OFTEN BETTER

What does this mean, using technology to do things we couldn't do before, and not just to do old things better? Too many of our children still struggle to achieve basic literacy and math skills, so how can high-concept technology projects really help them in ways that extra practice with pencil and paper, readers, and multiplication tables couldn't? Is flashy multimedia a good educational tool if it helps kids learn, or is it really just a needless distraction from the basics, a distraction whose cost is justified in the name of the computer-driven future? A good place to start looking for answers is with Cohen and his colleagues at Bank Street and the Center for Children and Technology and the concept of *ubiquitous tools*, a term frequently used in the world of technology but here applied to specific educational uses of common computer applications.

About five years ago, Bank Street began work on a project with the goal, as Cohen says, "to infuse technology into teacher education in diverse and 'inclusive' settings." In short, Cohen and his colleagues were charged with the broad task of leveraging technology to aid teaching and learning—and, in true school-reform spirit—to do so in settings that reflected the breadth of what teachers were really faced with in classrooms: first graders and sixth graders, high-level readers and those with severe learning disabilities, visual, kinesthetic, and auditory learners. In 1998, the college undertook Project EXPERT (EXPanding Educational Repertoire through Technology) with, as Cohen is quick to point out, "generous support from Atlantic Philanthropies to support the faculty's integration of technology into their teacher education classes."

Bank Street College has always held to the philosophy that its own faculty should serve as models for the graduate students they're training; what better way to learn to teach than by modeling the good practices of your own teachers? As part of an institution-wide reformation of the early elementary education degree program curriculum, the faculty was charged with the task of reshaping their courses and teaching practices to incorporate the use of technology in supporting learning.

Project EXPERT drew upon partnerships with outside individuals and institutions, especially the Center for Children and Technology. (I'd be remiss not to mention Dr. Cohen's insistence that his work "lives on the shoulders of giants, namely Jan Hawkins, Margaret Honey, and other colleagues at CCT.") As Cohen and Cornelia Brunner, associate director for CCT, wrote in their paper recounting the first year of EXPERT:

> The program called for graduate school faculty to learn to use technology as a tool in their own classrooms and to redesign their courses, supervised fieldwork experiences, and students' culminating projects to effectively use technology. The goals of Project EXPERT were to prepare classroom teachers to use technology wisely with their students and to provide leadership in their schools in the area of instructional technology and assessment. However, technology in itself was not the ultimate goal; it was used to serve the college's broader mission of preparing students to teach in diverse and inclusive settings. Unlike other models for technology integration that consisted primarily of supporting "islands of innovation"—individual faculty members who experiment with integrating technology into a specific course—Bank Street's Project EXPERT was a whole-school model for technology integration in the context of curricular reform.[2]

"During the first year we did it all wrong," Cohen laughed as he recounted the project's history. "We had a group of our 'critical friends' serve as evaluators for the project, and they told us that we basically missed the boat during that first year." But the team learned from its mistakes and reshaped its initial vision into a list of the four main goals of integrating technology literacy into the college's mission of teacher education. As the review paper explains:

> The goals for the program were redefined. The broad goal of infusing technology into the curriculum proved to be too broad and vague. As the first year came to a close, the project's leadership team, with the help of CCT, proposed to the faculty a goal of graduating students with the following skills:
>
> 1. Using the web as a tool for deepening research and inquiry
> 2. Using dialogue and exchange tools for engaging student learning
> 3. Authoring in multimedia in student constructive [*sic*] projects
> 4. Digital literacy: Finding and evaluating educational software.[3]

The first year of EXPERT may have been less successful than Cohen had hoped for, but from its failures arose a definitive direction for the future. With the help of CCT and a "very supportive" dean, Pat Wasley, the team regrouped and the project progressed into its second year. Cohen remembers: "Our critical friends told us to be more realistic. We therefore decided that we would help faculty rethink their courses so that teacher candidates would experience the use of technology in the service of their own learning."

The response is what would evolve into Project DEEP (DEepening and Expanding Project EXPERT) a three-year, million-dollar, federally funded project that was part of the larger Preparing Tomorrow's Teachers to use Technology (PT[3]) program. PT[3] is a U.S. Department of Education–sponsored grant program whose grantees work "to ensure that new teachers enter the classroom prepared to effectively use the computers that await them."[4]

The program has administered over four hundred grants since 1999 to fund projects ranging from professional development and course restructuring to the development of electronic student portfolios and video case studies for student teachers. PT[3] has also funded the development of national technology standards for teachers and students by the International Society for Technology Education (ISTE).[5] Cohen called PT[3] "one of the best federally funded projects I've seen."

The premise behind DEEP was simple enough: send Bank Street College faculty members into elementary school classrooms. Each faculty member would take four diverse learners from her classroom and use technology to teach them. Find out what works and what doesn't, and repeat the process armed with knowledge of your predecessors' efforts. A simple idea, but one that valued the individual participant's abilities to recognize a classroom need and fashion creative solutions that make good use of technology to support the learning of all students, not just those who may have already shown an interest in technology or aptitude for audiovisual learning.

So what happened? Two of Cohen's favorite examples of the project's success come from first- and second-grade classrooms:

Videotaping a Field Trip

A Bank Street College faculty member gave first and second graders video cameras and taught them the basics of shooting footage. The students were studying the Hudson River and they took the cameras with them on a field trip to the river. They conducted interviews on the bus on the way over to the river, asking their peers and teachers what they expected to see once when they arrived. Once at the river, the students documented their exploration of the site. Using the cameras helped facilitate students' thinking about what the river might look like *before* they'd actually seen it, as well as attempting to describe the river to a listener (on the bus) who couldn't actually see it, both of which are characteristic of Piaget's concrete operational stage of development in six- to twelve-year-olds.[6] Watching the tape then allowed for direct comparison between those predictions of what the river would look like and what it actually did look like.

Using PowerPoint to Support Multiple Learning Styles

Another Bank Street College faculty member worked with a second-grade class that was also studying the river. He assisted students in creating a six-slide slideshow in PowerPoint using hyper- and multimedia (audio and web links) to support their presentation. The students created an online glossary for hard vocabulary words like "estuary." One of the students was a girl who had language difficulties. For her contributions to the glossary, rather than typing the entries, she recorded herself speaking the definitions aloud. "This is a good example of using technology to serve different learning styles," Cohen explains. "This girl had trouble processing language so she spoke the definitions instead. The technology let us use her audio clips in the glossary. That's a great feature of PowerPoint that people forget—it supports audio, and that can be a powerful tool for students who have trouble with reading."

Neither of these examples is necessarily what software makers or politicians would point to as glitzy, attention-grabbing examples of cutting-edge technology in action, but perhaps they should be. In both cases, the technology fits into the classroom, aids rather than impedes learning, and supports diverse learners—the goals of Project DEEP.

In the second case, the technology's capacity to convey the same information via multiple means (thus supporting multiple learning styles) is simply and powerfully shown in the use of both written and spoken glossary entries. And it's worth noting that the glitz of the technology doesn't steal the show from the true worth of the lesson—what the kids learned about the river. "The PowerPoint project lived alongside poetry and a papier-mâché map of the river," Cohen remembered. "The computer didn't get all of the attention, but that's the way we like it."

Also worth pointing out is the choice of technologies in these two projects: videotape and PowerPoint. Most of you reading this are already familiar with both, and that familiarity is a key ingredient to the success of any technology-driven project. If the participants in a project aren't familiar with the medium they're being asked to work in, they have to tackle learning to use the medium before they can even begin to think about the content of the project itself.

In other words, if I'm trying to teach a unit on fractions using computer software, I have to learn how to operate the software before I can evaluate its usefulness in supporting my teaching of the unit. If the software is unfamiliar to me, or even worse, looks like nothing I've ever used before, this can be a very time-consuming and frustrating investment.

The computer industry is a fast-moving world full of technical jargon and rapid innovation. Daily announcements are made proclaiming "the next big thing," most of which turn out to be the next "no big deal." Talking to the average person on the street about secure socket layers, 128-bit encryption, and level-zero RAID storage is like speaking a foreign language. We're in an age where more and more people each day are finding out that, say, they can bank online. They want to know if it's safe to enter their checking and credit card account numbers into a website. But they don't know—and, rightly, don't care—that the aforementioned troika of web-server technology has something to do with the answer.

Just as consumers are beginning to buy into the notion that online banking can be safe and convenient, educators are beginning to understand that computers are here to stay, and that they can and should be incorporated into teaching practices—Internet-connected computers in particular. And just as you or I shouldn't have to learn a programming language in order to balance our checkbooks via the Net, we shouldn't be expected to learn to navigate overly complicated software in order to support our unit on fractions, either. Banks that want to bring their services online are doing so via standard web browsers because the widespread technology is becoming easier to access and use. Educators looking to bring technology into their teaching should similarly turn to ubiquitous tools.

EVERYBODY'S DOING IT, SO WHY SHOULDN'T YOU?

When the president of the United States wants to address the nation, he takes to the airwaves. Radio and television are our society's primary means of instantaneous mass communication. Lots of people get their news through newspapers and, increasingly, the Internet, but TV and radio are still the ways to go when it comes to the furthest reaching of mass communications. Television and radio are what we might call ubiquitous tools. We (mostly) all know how to use, and have access to, them. The president, therefore, can be safe in the assumption that his message will reach the people when he goes live on the air.

Marvin Cohen and the folks at Bank Street College like to refer to the concept of ubiquitous tools when talking about how to use technology in the classroom. Like much of what finds large-scale success in our world, theirs is a simple idea: use the tools people are already familiar with to teach them something new. If you're writing software to help teachers teach a unit on fractions, use graphics, symbols, metaphors, and methods they'll already be familiar with. Furthermore, model the way your software operates on the workings of software (or noncomputerized tools) they might already be familiar with.

The two elementary-level projects cited from Project DEEP worked, in part, because they made good use of ubiquitous tools. The first tool—television—is truly ubiquitous. Even if we've never shot, edited, and postproduced a TV show, most of us have at least used a TV and VCR, and maybe even a camcorder. There was no learning curve involved for first graders or their teachers in understanding the basics of what television is and how it can be used. Sure, the kids had to be taught to operate the cameras, but that's developing understanding on more of a mechanical than conceptual level.

The idea that we can record something from life and play it back over and over again on a monitor is already commonplace to these kids and their teachers. Most of them have access to a TV and VCR, as well. So this project can be undertaken and its results shared with others without much worry about whether everyone has the tools to be involved. (We can thank the triumph of VHS over Beta for some of that.) And though it wasn't yet possible when the experiment was initially carried out, the final video products from a project like this could now be shared with other educators, students, and their families via digital video posted to the web.

The tool employed in the second example is PowerPoint. PowerPoint is a piece of software that the Microsoft Corporation developed to help businesspeople make presentations to their bosses and clients. Microsoft might also have had teachers, students, lecturers, and television news writers in mind when they designed PowerPoint, but they probably weren't out to create a cultural phenomenon that has changed the way we think and communicate. That's what happened, though.[7]

PowerPoint, along with its even more famous sibling Microsoft Word, has become a ubiquitous tool within the world of personal computing. If you're comfortable on a home computer and have ever written anything that includes bullet points or text displayed over a two-tone color background, odds are you've encountered PowerPoint. If you've used a word processor in the past ten years, odds are it was Word.

Word and PowerPoint—along with e-mail and web browsers—are ubiquitous tools for personal computer users. Most home computers now come out of the box with some form of e-mail, web browsing, and text-editing software preinstalled. Most people's first software purchase beyond that is Microsoft Word (or the entire MS Office suite, which includes Word and PowerPoint). In addition, almost any school or workplace computer that's being kept relatively current will have all of the above available to its users.

Without getting into a long-winded treatise on the morality of Microsoft's domination of the consumer software market, it is worth mentioning that while there are other options out there, most home and school computers use Microsoft versions of all four ubiquitous tools: Word, PowerPoint, Outlook/Outlook Express (e-mail), and Internet Explorer (web). Word files, in particular, have become the industry standard for text documents much as VHS became synonymous with videotape in the 1980s and early 1990s.[8]

The Internet has made ubiquitous tools all the more important to thinking about how to leverage technology in your teaching. That is, because the tools themselves have become standardized, understood, and widely used, assignments and syllabi can be posted to a class website, homework can be e-mailed from student to teacher and back again, and educators can share and confer about best practices in online forums.

In the case of ubiquitous computing tools for education, what's important is not the brand name or particulars of the software itself, but rather the fact that we're using these tools regularly enough that they're becoming familiar to us. E-mail, web browsing, word processing, and creating multimedia presentations—these are the things the computer allows us to do that matter the most. You and your students are already familiar with the tools that do these jobs, or you will be soon.

HOW TO USE YOUR DIGITAL TOOLBOX

Great, so you've got access to these digital tools and want to start putting them to work. But how and why should you use them? First, it's important to bear in mind that incorporating technology into your teaching just because you feel like you should is the wrong way to go about it. Lots of educators in American schools have started coming under pressure in the past few years to use technology. School districts are allocating funds for new computers and network infrastructure in their budgets, and administrators want to see some results. But technology alone is never enough.

Dropping a computer lab blindly into a school and asking teachers to use it to somehow make their students smarter is like giving those teachers hammers and chisels and asking them to use those tools to improve education. Technology is a tool. It's an increasingly powerful, versatile tool, but it's still a tool—a *means* and not an end to improving teaching and learning. Effective use of technology requires thoughtful planning just like any other long-term undertaking.

Technology-minded politicians and administrators like to talk about bringing Internet access to schools as the first big step toward giving our children a future in a knowledge-driven world. The Internet *is* a very powerful means of broadcasting and gathering information. Much of what's available on the Net, however, is in no way specifically designed for use in educational settings—particularly when it comes to teaching children or anyone with less-than-fully developed literacy skills. In the future, more and more of what's available online will be true multimedia, innovatively designed combinations of video, animation, still photos, audio, and text (and, eventually, tactile and olfactory feedback) that immerse the users' senses in information.

Today, though, the vast majority of what's on the Internet is text. And if you can't read, you can't process text. You can't search, you can't filter results, and you can't possibly hope to separate reliable sources from biased or unreliable ones if you can't read (or interpret) words on the screen. Beyond that, if you can't type, you're going to have problems using the computer as well—for all the promises of voice recognition software and other input systems of the future, today's computers by and large depend on alphanumeric keyboards to get their instructions from human beings.[9]

So, while the notion of giving Internet access to a school full of struggling, middle school students in a poor neighborhood is a great one, the power of that gesture will be lost if steps aren't taken *before* teachers and students are let loose in the lab to conduct Internet research. Research has shown that proper preplanning and thought given to how technology can enhance a lesson plan (and not the other way around) greatly increases the chance of teachers and students alike getting value out of their use of technology in the classroom.[10]

That said, there are many great ways to leverage technology in your classroom without rewriting all of your lesson plans or reforming your entire school district. As stated in the outset of this book, the Internet is a vast, constantly growing reference base of human knowledge.

Unlike a print book or library, the Net also provides the means for dynamic communication with the authors of that knowledge. Although every person who's ever authored or been quoted in an online document may not be ready and willing to exchange e-mail with you, many websites provide e-mail addresses and scheduled opportunities to chat live with their knowledge makers.

Cohen recounted a successful Bank Street graduate class in which students read a text and then had e-mail access to the book's author for the next week. The author lived out of state, and arranging for her to spend a week in person with the students was impossible, but the convenience of e-mail made for the next best thing. Students were able to directly address questions that had arisen from their reading, while the author was able to become a resource for them without much impedance on the rest of her life. The college, in turn, was able to provide dialogue between students, text, and author while keeping its costs to a manageable minimum.

Providing access to experts is one powerful way in which educators can leverage the Internet to their students' benefit. Just as teachers have long invited guest speakers to address their classes in person, arranging for a live chat or e-mail conversation between students and authors, newsmakers, or other subject experts is a great way to bring learning to life.

Many nonprofit and commercial educational companies have taken this idea one step further by offering educational programs that incorporate webcasts by experts in the field. Archaeologists at a dig site in Egypt, for example, will exhibit their efforts and answer questions from fifth graders in Oklahoma via online videoconferencing. Researchers at sea can broadcast photographs and converse via text and audio chat with oceanography students back on the mainland. Astronauts can even communicate with classrooms from outer space.[11]

Whether it's a one-time online conference with the town mayor to augment your class's study of local government, an e-mail exchange with the author of a novel you're teaching, or an entire curriculum devoted to following a research team across a faraway land while you study the culture and history of that country, using the Net to bring guest speakers into your classroom is a great way to enhance the impact of what you're already teaching your students.

Conducting research using the Net is obviously a use of technology high on many educators' lists right now. The Net is a great research tool offering a wealth of resources, the majority of which can be used free of charge. Conducting proper online research with students does require extra preparation on the teacher's part, though. Just as you have to learn to weed out good information from bad when conducting your own web research, educators need to take the extra step of preselecting reliable and age-appropriate sites when designing an online research activity. Just as you do you not want your students taking bad information for the truth, neither do you want them lost in a sea of poorly written or overly difficult material that may frustrate them to the point of losing interest in the topic altogether.

For example, let's say you're designing a research activity for a fifth-grade Earth science lesson. Think about designing the lesson without the use of the Net; what source materials will you point your students to? Elementary or low-middle-school textbooks, maybe some videos or periodicals like *National Geographic Explorer* (the children's version of *National Geographic* magazine). You're not going to give your kids college-level geology textbooks or professional research journals, are you? No, of course not. They probably won't be able to make heads or tails of the scientific writing and jargon, let alone the advanced concepts that mean little to a ten-year-old.

The same idea holds true when designing a lesson that uses online resources. Turning your students loose to type "fossils" into a Google search will yield a plethora of results, but there's no telling which will be appropriate for your third graders and their reading levels. Just as you preselect textbooks and other "old media" resources to suit your subject matter and your students' comprehension levels, so too must you preselect websites that will be appropriate to your class's abilities and interests. Find some good sites with text and graphics explaining how fossils are made and limit students' research to those sites only. Not only will you cut down on time wasted searching for good sites, you'll also increase the chances that the subject engages your students and inspires them to learn.

Furthermore, studies such as CCT's report on the Intel Teach to the Future program have shown that ineffective web research can actually lead to increased plagiarism. Students who come across overly difficult material while looking for online resources are prone to cutting and pasting material that they don't understand directly into their work, attempting to pass it off as their own. Clipboard functionality built into Windows and Macintosh operating system software facilitates easy copying of text from web pages into word-processing documents.

In one study, students suspected of plagiarizing from websites were asked to read aloud and explain the material in question. Many of them couldn't pronounce some of the words they claimed to have written and eventually confessed to having copied entire passages blindly into their work from online sources, or even resorted to making information up entirely and trying to pass it off as culled from various websites.[12]

This is the kind of incident that leads some to protest the use of the Internet in schools and classrooms. "Children are being taught lies!" they say.

"They plagiarize instead of thinking for themselves because the computer makes it too easy!" This is simply not true. The problem in cases like this is not that the software makes it too easy to cut and paste text between programs; the problem lies in the way the activity was designed and carried out.

Students should never be made to research using materials that they can't understand—it's the educator's job to select appropriate resources for their students, whether they're textbooks, websites, or anything else. A carefully selected web resource given in lieu of a blind search directive may not make every student love geology, but it will do a lot to avoid failures like the one described above. Yes, there's a lot of inaccurate or misleading information online, but there's also a lot of great stuff out there. The trick is to separate the good from the bad. Educational technology companies stake their claim on doing that work for you, the educator. Until your students have developed the critical thinking and information literacy skills to conduct effective searches on their own, the responsibility of finding good resources for them before they sit down to the screen lies squarely with you.

EXTENDING YOUR CLASSROOM USING THE INTERNET

My first year as a teacher was an eye-opener for me in many ways. I had always been one of the most tech-savvy of my peer group, what with my computer consulting job, myriad electronic gadgets with me wherever I went, and state-of-the-art Macintosh on my desk at home. But the gadgets alone weren't bringing me the satisfaction I craved from my work, so I turned to teaching as a way to share my interest in technology with others.

The beginning of my teaching career coincided with my enrollment in a master's program in educational technology in New York City. One of the first courses I took was History of Communications, a historical overview of the technology of communication and the theories of intellectual and social development that grew out of the landmark advances in that technology. As you might guess from the opening chapter of this book, that course has had a long-lasting impact on my life and work.

The course met one night a week, and the enrollment cut a fairly wide swath through the technology-minded educational community of the time. There were veteran teachers preparing (by choice or mandate) to take on new roles as school and district technology coordinators, and their colleagues who were preparing to leave the schoolhouse to develop software for educational publishing houses. Middle-aged technology professionals interested in trying their hands in the classroom sat next to fresh-faced twenty-year-olds enrolled in the full-time preservice program. Some came straight from long days in front of thirty-plus student classrooms in the outer reaches of the city, drawing on endless reserves of energy to share their experiences and views with the foreign students who sat in the back of the room, silently taking in the lectures and discussions.

Student grades in History of Communications, as explained on the syllabus, would be determined by consideration of several factors: written responses to weekly readings, completion of three major written papers, midterm and final assignments, participation in class discussions, and participation in online discussions. Nothing so out of the norm until you get to that last item in the list: participation in online discussions.

History of Communications was one of a small handful of Teachers College courses at the time to make use of computer-mediated discussion groups to extend dialogue beyond the physical and time constraints of the classroom. Most of the students in the educational technology program were working teachers and other professionals who commuted from day jobs in all parts of the city (and beyond into the suburbs) for evening classes. Finding the time to get to a few evening classes each week, let alone tackling reading and homework assignments, was task enough for these students, many of whom had homes, families, and yes, stacks of their own students' papers to deal with at the end of the day.

Set up as a text-only discussion group on one of the campus servers, the History of Communications online forum filled the gap between a large group of people and a shortage of time with which they could talk to one another. Users could log on to the forum from computers on campus or virtually anywhere else, allowing the discussion to be picked back up during a break in the work day, a weekend study session, or late on a weeknight when the kids, spouse, and family dog were tucked away in bed.

Upon entering the forum, you would see a chronological overview of posts to the discussion board, listed by user name and subject header. Students could select the messages they wanted to view in full, skipping over those they'd read already or weren't interested in. Replies to existing messages were marked by subject headers beginning with "Re:" (e.g., "Re:

Noah's misunderstanding of postmodernism"), and quoting previous posts or starting new subjects from scratch were also options.[13]

Participation in the online discussion was mandatory, but only to a small degree — students were required to post an introductory greeting and a small handful of messages over the duration of the semester. What actually happened in the online discussion was pretty remarkable: it grew like wildfire right off the bat. I think our professor posted once or twice at the beginning of the semester to get the ball rolling, and that was the last we heard from him. Students carried the discussion, picking up on questions and ideas posed during in-person class meetings, discussing aspects of the texts not covered in person, and raising new themes arising from various aspects of any and all of the above.

Not everyone took to the online format; some people had a hard time expressing themselves in writing, adjusting to the technology, or simply weren't interested in giving time to the course beyond the minimum required of them. Others, however, seemed to find comfort in "talking on the computer" that they didn't find in a live class setting. Whether it was the time this format afforded to composing and editing one's thoughts that couldn't be found speaking in class or just the simple fact of not having to speak in front of a room full of strangers, certain members of the class who never spoke in person began to fill the online forum with theories, criticism, and questions that lent a great deal to our explorations of the material at hand.

After a few weeks, patterns started to emerge in the discussions. Some new topics would lead to long discussions while others would peter out after only a few replies. Group conversations would grow between three, four, or five people, extending to many messages on a given topic, while debates kept between pairs of students would weave themselves in and out of these larger conversations. Dialogue grew between certain pairs and groups of people as they found themselves on the same — or opposite — sides of various fences. "Lurkers" abounded, I'm sure, reading messages that interested them but refraining from comment, like their silent counterparts in the physical classroom. After a few weeks of using the online forum, in fact, I found myself looking around the room during in-person class meetings, wondering which faces matched up with which names and postings on the online forum.

While this sort of electronic discussion group may not be appropriate for all classes and situations — it won't, for instance, add very much to a junior high school math class that meets five times a week—it can be an effective way to use technology to extend the classroom setting beyond the constraints traditionally imposed by time and physical meeting places.

The format can be empowering both for learners who naturally express themselves more easily in writing than by speaking aloud and also those who might feel shy about speaking up in a large class setting. Furthermore, in a situation like the class described in which class meetings are limited to an hour or two a week for the teacher to review old material, introduce new topics, and mediate discussion, a newsgroup-type setting can really allow for more in-depth discussion than could otherwise be possible.

While the importance of face-to-face discussion of critical material cannot be overemphasized, extending the discussion into an arena accessible to students at their convenience can really be a boon to encouraging participation, not to mention getting to know classmates a little better.

Online educational discussions need not be limited to institutes of higher education. Today's teenagers and preteens are flocking to chat rooms and instant messenger services in droves, using the Net to talk much as kids of my generation used the telephone.

Eighth graders I know regularly hang out in chat rooms together while doing homework much as I used to call a friend on the phone when I got stuck on a hard question. In fact, broadband Internet connections at home let today's kids talk on the phone to one of their friends while hanging out in chat rooms with several more at the same time. The practice of extending the student-teacher relationship beyond the walls of the classroom is an oft-debated topic within educational circles, and while I wouldn't go so far as to say high school teachers should be setting up chat rooms for their students to gossip in, there is the opportunity to provide additional educational support for your students via the Net.[14]

An oft-used and relatively easy way to extend your classroom beyond its four walls into cyberspace is by publishing a class website. In upper grades and college, class websites are often used to distribute syllabi, assignments, course readings, special notices, and reminders to students. Elementary schools will often use websites to keep parents up to date on school events and also display student work online.

Depending on your students' age and the availability of the Internet to them, you may wish to distribute all materials via the website instead of printing and handing them out in class (suitable for a college course) or just use it as a clearinghouse for nonessential reference and supplementary materials. As college campuses become universally wired to the Net, for example, professors are starting to find that posting lecture notes, links to additional web resources, and electronic copies of worksheets and other documents is an easy and useful way to leverage the web to their students' advantage. My mother, in fact, is just this year beginning to use the online teaching system at her university to electronically distribute syllabi, lecture notes, and materials to her graduate and undergraduate nurse practitioning students. I couldn't be prouder.

Taking things a step further, you may wish to open up new lines of communication with your students via e-mail exchanges or online "office hour" sessions in chat forums. Again, online communication is fast becoming part and parcel of how today's generation lives, so why not open yourself up to their "world," especially if you're not used to it?

Making yourself accessible to students through e-mail can be a great way to not only offer them extra help outside of the classroom but also an unobtrusive way to communicate with them. Just as an online forum can open up discussions to students who aren't comfortable debating with their fellow students in person, e-mail can be a less intimidating way for some students to feel comfortable talking to their teachers.

An e-mail from a teacher affords a student the opportunity to reply without some of the performance pressure associated with being called on in class—there's no demand for an instantaneous answer in front of a classroom of expectant peers. A student can take time replying to e-mail, compose and edit thoughts before replying, and often feel more at ease with doing so because of the casual nature of the medium.

Should you choose to make yourself available to students through e-mail or other electronic means, or to publish class materials to a website, be sure to do so with student equity foremost in mind. If Net access is not readily available for all of your students and its use is not a part of the course requirements, don't use the web for anything essential to what you're teaching. That is, if not all of your students can easily get online, offering extra resources on a website or carrying on occasional e-mail exchanges with students is probably fine, but you might want to think twice before holding online-only help sessions if some of your students literally can't get to them.

USING VIDEO TO TEACH

It's no secret that today's kids (and adults of my generation) are growing up on television. For many families, the TV has become a surrogate member, keeping us company when nobody else is awake or at home, entertaining us when we're bored or distressed, and providing our first link to the outside world through news and weather reports. Though television has progressed immensely from its introduction on giant black-and-white consoles a half-century ago to today's digital flat screens that grab hundreds of channels of programming from the heavens via satellite feeds, we have primarily looked at TV as a consumer medium since its inception. Television has traditionally been something that we watch, not something that we create and share with others.

This perception started to change in the 1990s with the advent of home video cameras. Camcorders, as they came to be known, took the idea of the home movie from the old filmstrip projector in the den and put it on the big screen in the living room. Over the past decade, advances in digital video technology have brought moving pictures to the personal computer. More and more new computers are being outfitted specifically for video recording and editing, putting the power of video production in consumers' hands. Computers can take video from a camcorder, VCR, or television signal, digitize it into files that are easily edited, and share via the web or record to tape or even digital video disc (DVD). Technology that was prohibitively complicated and expensive not ten years ago has been brought to home users by way of innovations like the MiniDV digital tape format and Apple's easy-to-use iMovie video-editing software.

Though the education industry as a whole tends to lag behind the business and consumer markets when it comes to adopting new technologies, educators themselves are a hearty and often adventurous bunch. We rely upon our standby methods and practices because we know them to work, but our passion for finding better ways to create understanding for our students does lead us to much experimentation when it comes to finding better ways to reach our students.

Since the invention of the VCR, teachers have been bringing audiovisual carts into their classrooms to show students videos pertaining to almost every educational subject you can think of. Videotapes can be a great way to enhance a lesson with primary source material or historical fiction, relate to younger students through a contemporary medium, or (like the uses of the Internet discussed before) bring a virtual guest speaker into the classroom.

The advent of digital video expands the applications of video in the classroom in two main ways. First, it allows for teacher and student production of video material. That is, it lets us make our own "home" movies for school. Second, it allows for individual or small-group viewing of video material on computers. For example, let's take a look at the implications of both of these points in classroom settings:

Using Digital Video for Case Studies

Hal Melnick is a professor of mathematics education at the Bank Street College: he teaches teachers how to teach math. Melnick is an advocate of the thoughtful use of technology in the classroom, and he's also a good example of Bank Street's philosophy that graduate faculty should be models of teaching to their students. In other words, Melnick should not only be sharing his ideas and techniques on teaching but he should be doing so in a manner upon which young teachers can model their own professional ways.

"There's been clear trend over the past two or three years in the adoption of video case study," Melnick said. "Math educators are now keenly interested in using video case studies. It offers new teachers images of excellent classroom practice. I chose to develop one such tool for early childhood teachers. It is one thing to read about how the Carolyn Pratt Unit Blocks are essential for developing a five-year-old's geometric knowledge and quite something else to watch a child plan and construct a symmetrical masterpiece on video."

Melnick's own Math for Teachers course at Bank Street leverages digital video to give his students access to best practices via video case studies. His classroom is set up with viewing stations that place small groups of students around laptops loaded with case studies in digital video form. The students watch the videos on the computer screens, and have the ability to rewind, replay, and otherwise control the playback to suit their pace of learning.

"This affords the simplicity of watching the playback over and over again, but with small-group control," Melnick explains. "It's much better than having me at the front of the room with one monitor that everyone watches at the same time." The software also allows the students to take

notes on the computer as they watch, which "allows for interaction between you and the document and even the author."

"Hal's videos allow our students to see math through the eyes of a
four-year-old," explains Dr. Cohen. "They serve as examples in action,
home movies of really interesting teaching practices." The digital format
allows instructors to compile many practices onto CDs, which can easily
be distributed to students to watch on their own. Of course, the videos
can also be distributed over the Internet to broadband users, a project that
Bank Street is currently working on.

"We're building a local knowledge base to put faculty's work online to
share with each other and new teachers," he says. Every good teacher knows
the value in sharing with and learning from other teachers, from building on
ideas to discovering the value of something you've never thought of before.

The easy-to-use simplicity of new video-editing software has been
paramount to the success of digital video as a means for sharing teaching
practices among faculty and students. "We couldn't use video without
iMovie," Cohen explains. "The faculty wouldn't put up with what you
need to [do to] edit VHS. Now they edit."

Teaching Literacy through Video

Another successful and deceptively simple project from Bank Street was
on display at a graduate student technology fair I visited early in the winter 2003 semester. Olivia Jones, a graduate student in the early childhood
education program, worked with a first-grade student in one of her student
teaching placements. This girl was a beginning/emerging reader, struggling but desperately wanting to read.

In one of their sessions, Jones and her student read a beginning reader
in which the main character celebrates the things she can do: "I can dress
myself," "I can tie my own shoes," "I can feed the dog," and so on. Jones
then videotaped her student doing some of the things she does in her daily
life: tying her shoes, riding her scooter, reading a book.

They then watched the video together and Jones had her student write
one-sentence captions describing each scene. Jones then loaded the video
onto a laptop using iMovie and they worked together to add the captions
into the movie as graphical subtitles. The student also recorded the captions as a voice-over narration. They then had their very own *I Can* movie,
of which the student was the star.

Jones said that what made the project work was a combination of the excitement of the student getting to make a movie about herself and the simplicity of the technology involved. The point was to encourage the development of reading and writing skills, not to learn the ins and outs of video editing, and iMovie's user-friendliness kept the technology out of the way of learning. Having a fun goal to strive for—in this case, making a movie, of which both student and teacher now have videotape copies— kept the student excited about learning, and the final project clearly shows her pride in both being onscreen and having improved her language skills enough to write the captions herself.

SIMPLE TECHNOLOGY FOSTERS POWERFUL IDEAS

As the technology available to us becomes more and more powerful, we can (and will) be able to use it to take on increasingly complex tasks. Increased computing power has brought video editing to the consumer by way of programs like iMovie, which take advantage of powerful processors and very sophisticated programming. The key to iMovie's success, though, lies as much with the simplicity of its user interface as it does with the programming power that rests behind the controls.

As Cohen said, teachers wouldn't put up with what was required of them to edit video on old VHS machines. The first generation of computer-based video editors were at least that complicated. Were it not for the breakthrough of iMovie—the power of technology wedded to the simple elegance of a good user interface—teachers and students all over America wouldn't be starting to harness the enormous power of capturing, editing, and sharing video footage as part of their schoolwork.

Thanks to iMovie, Melnick's students share best practices by sharing videos on CDs. Furthermore, Jones helped a little girl improve her reading, writing, and confidence by shooting a movie and writing captions for it. The scientists at Apple Computer who wrote the code for iMovie may or may not have had these uses for their program in mind, but that's not their job. Their job is to come up with ideas for new technologies and make the ideas come to life in the way of hardware and software. Our job as educational technologists is to come up with ideas for new ways to use that hardware and software to help our students learn.

LOGO, Word, PowerPoint, the Internet, iMovie—these are the tools computer scientists are putting at our disposal and the world is adopting as the standards of communication for our new, connected world. Figuring out how PowerPoint can support multiple learning styles? That's where a good teacher steps in and works her own brand of magic.

As we move forward through history, communication technologies will only continue to grow in terms of their abilities to exchange more and more increasingly sophisticated information between a larger share of the world's peoples. Where once only the elite among men had the means to communicate via the written word, now we send home movies to one another from our wireless computers. Today's generation of learners—children in particular—are growing up on advanced communications technology and will increasingly rely upon electronic transmittal of text, audio, and video as the years go by.

We have a chance now, as educators at the forefront of the information revolution, to shape the ways in which students young and old think about these new technologies and how they can be used to shape the world for the better. Much as students have long been taught the value of reading and writing, so are we charged with teaching a new breed of learners not only how to use information technology but why they also need to think critically about its role in our world.

From yellow highlighters at the corner store to e-mails and digital movies sent across the world through the Internet, as scientists invent new technologies, we in turn must learn to use these tools first for ourselves and then again with our students' growth in mind. The results of our efforts will not only impact our students today, but so too will they live on as the groundwork upon which a new literacy is built—literacy in the information age.

NOTES

1. Originally housed on Bank Street in Manhattan's Greenwich Village neighborhood, the college moved uptown to West 112th Street in 1970 but retained its name despite the new address. For the complete history of the school, see http://www.bankstreet.edu/about/history.html

2. Marvin Cohen and Cornelia Brunner, *Integrating Technology into Teacher Education: A Review of Bank Street's Project EXPERT*, at http://www.ericsp.org/pages/digests/BankStreet.htm

3. Cohen and Brunner, *Integrating Technology*.

4. http://www.pt3.org

5. http://www.iste.org

6. Michael Cole and Sheila R. Cole, *The Development of Children*, 4th ed. (New York: Worth Publishers, 2001), 478.

7. For a fascinating look at the impact PowerPoint has had on the way we communicate, I suggest Ian Parker's article "Absolute PowerPoint: Can a Software Package Edit Our Thoughts?" in the May 20, 2001, issue of the *New Yorker* magazine.

8. While MS Office certainly isn't the only office productivity suite available to computer users, it has become the industry standard. PC users may rely on WordPerfect or other word processors for their home use, while Macintosh devotees may be used to AppleWorks or ClarisWorks software instead of MS Office. However, Microsoft's technical and marketing strategies, along with the widespread adoption of sending files electronically via e-mail, have made MS Word and its .doc file format ubiquitous when it comes to word processing.

9. This is not in any way to trivialize the important and innovative work being done around the globe in the field of assistive technology for disabled persons. Rather, the reality is that the vast majority of computers being used in educational situations today are "standard issue" PCs reliant upon keyboards and mice for input. Many educators and students do not know about alternative I/O solutions for the disabled or do not have the resources to make use of them. See below for related resources.

10. Wendy Martin et al., *An Evaluation of Intel® Teach to the Future: Year Two Final Report*, Center for Children and Technology (September 2002), 11–12.

11. Classroom Connect (http://www.classroomconnect.com) is well known for their *Quest* series of online expeditions/webcasts. A host of other companies, including One World Journeys (http://www.oneworldjourneys.com) and nonprofit and government agencies such as NASA (http://education.nasa.gov/) also host online expeditions.

12. Martin et al., *An Evaluation*, p. 16.

13. This type of discussion forum, while new to many of the students in the class at the time, had long since caught on among early adopters of the Net as a favored way to hold *asynchronous* group conversations. The technology employed is relatively low tech, and the use of plain text for reading and writing posts makes the medium accessible to even the lowest-bandwidth Internet users. Today, USENET discussion groups—newsgroups—number in the tens of thousands, covering almost every topic imaginable, from academics to entertainment, politics to sports, and everything in between. For more information, try connecting to http://groups.google.com

14. Research into the effects of computer-mediated communications and "virtual reality" on our social and intellectual lives is developing into an important area of modern psychology and sociology. A great place to start for more in-depth exploration of the subject is Sherry Turkle's *Life on the Screen*, a well-researched and fascinating book that follows people's journeys between their online and "real" lives.

SUGGESTED READING

Michael Cole and Sheila R. Cole, *The Development of Children*, 4th ed. (New York: Worth Publishers, 2001).

Howard Rheingold, *The Virtual Community: Homesteading on the Electronic Frontier* (New York: Harper Perennial, 1994).

———. *Smart Mobs: The Next Social Revolution* (Cambridge, Mass.: Perseus, 2002).

SUGGESTED WEB LINKS

Bank Street College of Education, http://www.bankstreet.edu
Center for Applied Special Technology (CAST), http://www.cast.org
Center for Children and Technology (CCT), http://www.edc.org/cct
The International Society for Technology Education (ISTE), http://www.iste.org
Preparing Tomorrow's Teachers to Use Technology (PT[3]), http://www.pt3.org
A Universal Design for Learning, http://www.cast.org/udl

Digital Video

Apple iMovie, http://www.apple.com/imovie
2-pop Digital Filmmaker's Forum, http://www.2-pop.com

Chapter Five

Literacy in the Internet Age

REDEFINING LITERACY

Understanding even the customary criteria for evaluating the value and relevance of traditional media production is becoming more critical as raw, unedited, unsolicited information enters the classroom via the Internet. Teachers who have been able to rely on publishers, editors, curriculum directors, and master teachers to select appropriate materials for them can still do so, but the degree of control they have over what information their "wired" students are exposed to is seriously curtailed. Now they need new criteria and useful strategies to help these students make positive and constructive use of that information.[1]

When I was in high school, I had a government teacher named Mr. Evans. Mr. Evans was something of a rabble-rouser in my sleepy suburban town—he was often in trouble with the school district for challenging norms and policies he found unfair or offensive, and got himself in slightly bigger trouble a few times for speaking out on various issues in the school and town newspapers. He was the kind of guy who would say something controversial to make a point in the name of free speech to teach his students a lesson, even if he knew he'd be explaining himself over and over again later, and some people would still never get the point. Mr. Evans liked shock value, and while I didn't always agree with his methods, he had the best interests of his students at heart and I admired his gumption and principles.

Mr. Evans was also very intelligent and well versed in American history and government. There were rumors that he'd been in the CIA before becoming a teacher, though outlandish rumors about teachers tend to be as common as spiral-bound notebooks in a high school. He did, however, ascribe to that one supposed tenet of the CIA that's always bandied about in spy movies: nothing is as it seems.

Mr. Evans taught his students to look closely at things and to take a second, even closer, pass at anything being passed off as the truth; he taught us to think critically and carefully. Just because something is written in a textbook—or a newspaper, for that matter—doesn't mean it's the truth, he said. In fact, the more persistent people are about insisting there's a "clear truth" or only one side to a story, the more likely you are to find some interesting bit of contradictory information by digging around a little.

In his classroom, Mr. Evans taught students about the relationships between government and information, media, and power. What he wanted us to take from his class was a cursory knowledge of the facts of the modern history of American government bolstered by the beginnings of a more complex understanding of how that government works. "It's all about the relationships between things," he would say, "the relationships between people and institutions, institutions and other institutions, power and other powers."

His assignments and methods of assessment strongly reflected his belief in the importance of understanding these relationships. What mattered to him most was our showing that we understood the information and how different pieces of it related to one another. Showing that we could follow the conventions of essay writing was secondary to showing that we understood the material and could think critically about it. Essays were welcomed responses to assignments, but so were flowcharts, diagrams, and almost anything else that could be justified as an appropriate means of expressing our thinking.

Not everyone in the class caught on to Mr. Evans's brand of thinking, let alone his mode of expression. He wanted us to break free from the traditional ways of thinking and writing that had been impressed upon our brains during ten years of schooling, but perhaps didn't lend quite enough guidance when it came to showing us just how to do that. Still, though I may have been confused by Mr. Evans's class almost as much as I was inspired by it, I took two very important lessons away from it.

One, every bit of information we receive in this world comes prepackaged with the slant of its author, no matter how objective that author claims to be. And two, learning to understand and communicate information is just about the most important skill we can hope to acquire and master in our lives. Learning to read and write should be at the top of most people's list, but these are not the only viable ways of expression that we have.

This chapter takes a look at the value of multiple forms of literacy and expression in the Internet age. The vast majority of information available to us still comes in written form, whether it's published via print or electronic means. The ability to read and write with a degree of competence is the cornerstone of success in a world made from thoughts and ideas, and often is paramount to gaining the means to express oneself in a variety of other ways: job seekers must be able to write cover letters and résumés, educators and visual artists need to write grants to obtain funding for their work, and so on. However, the abilities to process and create new forms of visual and other media are fast becoming important components of the new literacy.

DIGESTING OUR MULTIMEDIA DIET

Modern life is saturated with information broadcast in a multitude of ways. Every day we are fed a steady diet of multimedia, from music videos to talk radio, from illustrated billboards to animated television programs. Urban dwellers feel it more than their rural brethren, as the 21st-century city is literally for sale to the highest bidder, with advertisers taking full advantage of every phone booth, bus stop, and taxicab to hawk their wares in technicolor. No matter where we are, though, the moment we pick up a newspaper or magazine, or turn on a television or radio, we are opening ourselves up to a stream of communication that demands a new form of literacy for understanding. Text is accompanied by sound, imagery, or both. Information comes at us in multiple forms at once. Professional media producers painstakingly craft their wares to inundate our senses with information at a rate approaching—or, often, deliberately achieving—overload.

For several decades television has been the ultimate form of multimedia information. Combining moving imagery with sound, broadcast technology quickly evolved to allow for color, multichannel audio, and then layers of video and motion graphics composited atop one another. Today's viewer is used to news or sports programming in which a split screen shows a main program (with sound), supplemented by one or more scrolling tickers of text updates, and perhaps a third graphical element. A news reader might be framed by scrolling headlines and stock prices on the bottom of the screen and an icon-based weather report on the right.

The Internet promises to take the multimedia format a step further than television, and in some cases already has. Even in today's still nascent form, broadband Internet applications allow for everything television does with the added component of user interactivity.

Where a television show limits viewer participation to changing the channel, an Internet application is literally just beginning with the canned content streamed to the user. Subsequent choices made by the user shape the next stages of the experience, whether they're digging deeper into the subject matter through the exploration of content, jumping off to a separate but related subject through links, or interacting with other visitors to the site through e-mail, chat, or bulletin board applications.[2]

In a world so dependent on the media for information, entertainment, and communication, is it enough to rely on our common sense and instincts to make sense of it all? Consider the daily barrage of text, imagery, and sound that broadcasters, publishers, and advertisers unleash upon us. Does our training in the "three Rs" of reading, writing, and arithmetic sufficiently equip us to make sense of sound bites and scrolling text headlines projected on the screens that shadow us nearly everywhere we go? As educators, does our responsibility to students in this brave new world of multimedia end with teaching them to read books and write well-constructed paragraphs?

No. Reading and writing are the cornerstones of education, but they are no longer enough. Learning to live in the information age requires a new form of literacy on the parts of teachers and students alike, a literacy that extends beyond the written word into still and moving imagery, streaming audio, and dynamic information. The cornerstone of literacy will still be the ability to work with text—encoding and decoding words as the basis of assessing and interpreting information—but life in the rapidly shifting Internet age requires a malleable, multimedia literacy to keep up with the times.

MEDIA SPECIALISTS AND MEDIA GENERALISTS

In their useful overview of the role of new media in the classroom, *The New Media Literacy Handbook*, Cornelia Brunner and William Talley of the Center for Children and Technology (CCT) address some of the issues and strategies important to educators who are trying to adapt to the changing media landscape in order to better serve their students. While many schools employ a computer or technology coordinator to manage computer hardware and software or a library media specialist in charge of audiovisual material and equipment (TVs, VCRs, and so on), these jobs have traditionally required much more in the way of organizational skills and technical facility than a pedagogical understanding of how to make the best use of multimedia in the classroom.

The media specialist can provide a teacher with videocassettes and instructions for using playback equipment, but won't necessarily be able to lend a hand when it comes to figuring out how to structure curriculum and lessons to create a suitable context within which to view the material. As Brunner and Talley put it:

> The most common organization of technology support in schools—the "media specialist" or "computer coordinator" who presides over the computer lab and has very little to do with teachers or curriculum—is a key barrier to successful technology integration. Schools need, instead, "media generalists"—staff members who are technically skilled but who are equally knowledgeable about curriculum and interpersonally skilled at working . . . around students' use of technologies for subject-matter learning.[3]

This notion of a media generalist is an important idea to consider. Teachers cannot be expected to keep abreast of all developments in new media and information technology. They can reasonably be asked to develop some facility with using the Internet and other ubiquitous tools as discussed in the previous chapter, but English and math teachers have enough to keep abreast of in their own fields without being asked to stay on top of the newest developments in digital technology. To that end, there is a real need in our schools for people with both an interest in and facility for technology, in addition to an understanding of how to help teachers use new media to become better teachers.

The ideal characteristics of the prototypical media generalist are not so different from those of the new media literate teacher, save for the thorough understanding of technology that subject matter teachers need not possess. Media literate teachers must be familiar enough with both the curricular content and media in question to understand what options are available for research and expression, not to mention which of these are appropriate within a given context.

That is to say, an English teacher presenting Shakespeare to her class should not only be aware that screening videotaped performances of *Hamlet* might help tenth graders better understand the play but also that some students might wish to submit a hypertext plot synopsis and family tree of the characters as a response to the play. In this case, the teacher should have some basis for deciding if such a project is appropriate, and if so, how it will be evaluated.

For example, some students might decide to liven up their hypertext with audio content. A presentation full of audio snippets lifted directly from the videotape watched in class may not show any real understanding of the play, whereas the same visual presentation augmented with original narration describing the characters' motivations, roles, and contemporaries in modern literature could be an effective way of using multimedia to underscore in-depth knowledge and understanding of the work. The "media generalist" can be of use to teachers and students in helping to brainstorm, create, and evaluate multimedia projects like this one.

The task of evaluating students' work in new media will surely be more daunting to some teachers than the students' assignment to create the work was to the students. Multimedia is a pretty loose term, and it's not at all uncommon for students as young as eight and nine to be more "tech savvy" than veteran teachers who've been doing just fine with blackboards, chalk, pencils, and paper for the past few decades. Assigning a multimedia project to a high school class armed with laptops, camcorders, and the Internet is, in the eyes of some educators, akin to opening a Pandora's box of unmanageable bells, whistles, and misguided energy. What could the children possibly do with pictures and sound that they couldn't do better with well-formed sentences, you might ask? And, even more frightening, how could I possibly make any sense of it?

PRIMARY SOURCES AND
THE CASE FOR VISUAL LITERACY

As part of the fourth-grade scope and sequence for social studies, students in New York City are expected to be familiar with a multitude of primary and secondary sources. As the guidelines read:

Using a variety of skills and strategies, by the end of the school year, students should . . . locate information by investigating different types of primary and secondary sources, such as: maps, globes, graphs, charts, newspapers, magazines, documents, historical fiction and nonfiction, timelines, cartoons, surveys, media, museums, interviews, diaries, posters, brochures, speeches, travel guides, the Internet, and other reference works.[4]

The difference between a primary and secondary source can be difficult to grasp, even for those of us well beyond the fourth grade. And learning to read and interpret every type of information from historical fiction to "media" and "the Internet" is a daunting task. What's important to point out here, however, is that while many of the types of documents listed above are partially or entirely text based, they also require different and specific vocabularies for successful decoding. A student asked to read a map must understand what a legend is and how to use it. Graphs and charts come in a plethora of styles specific to displaying various types of information, and students must be able to make sense of any and all of them. We educate students about these types of documents, train them to read them, and expect that they will be able to make use of this training in assessment situations.

Maps, charts, brochures, posters, timelines, and cartoons have been popular and reliable forms of information transmission over the last century, in large part because they are easily reproducible in print form. The printing press first made the widespread dissemination of text easy, and then simple line drawings and graphics. As news-gathering and remote publication technologies advanced over the course of the 20th century, the ease with which a graphic could be captured, transmitted, and reproduced in newspapers across the globe increased and the cost of the process of doing so decreased. The ratio of cost to technological advances evened out enough in the last quarter of the century to allow for the desktop publishing revolution, during which personal computers and copy machines gave schools, small businesses, and even home users the ability to publish, on a budget, periodicals chock-full of original text and artwork.

Photographs were something of a trickier business during this time because of the relative sophistication of the capture and publishing process involved with photography. Photographs don't photocopy nearly as easily as text and line art, even in black and white; before the digital camera revolution in the early 2000s, capturing a digital version of a photograph traditionally required developing the film and then scanning the print using an expensive computer scanner.

Digital cameras that download images directly to a computer have changed all of that, but even the most efficient of today's photo printers uses much more ink to reproduce a digital image than for printing text. Hence, mass-sharing photographic imagery through print is still best left to industrial publishers of books and periodicals, even though the individual can run off a thousand copies of a text-only newsletter on the cheap.

The Internet is changing that by removing print from the equation. Once you have a computer monitor in place, the price of displaying a single pixel is no less than the cost of showing a thousand more next to it. In other words, the high cost of printing sophisticated imagery is eliminated because there are no physical materials involved. The only costs associated with reproducing information online (beyond the initial investment of the computer itself) are those of storing and moving the information around and generating the electricity to make it all happen. Rendering a word onscreen costs the same amount as displaying an image, playing an audio file, or even showing a movie.

Of course, images, audio, and movies contain more data than words do, so there is the issue of storing all of that information. But ever more inexpensive storage media, advances in data compression (the mathematical process of condensing information into a smaller package for travel; think along the lines of packing a suitcase very tightly with only the clothes you really need), and the increasing speed with which data itself is pushed and pulled along Internet connections are making issues surrounding file sizes less and less of a problem.

All of this is to say that images are now, more than ever, an important part of the way we communicate. Massive databases of images old and new are available online, giving users access to everything from historical artifacts to stock photography. Digital cameras that can take pictures and transfer them to websites with the click of a button have become widespread to the point that a new generation of cell phones with integrated cameras is now on the streets. For decades, since the widespread adoption of newspapers, magazines, and television into our cultural commerce, we have been gobbling up pictures as fast as publishers can sell them to us. In the years immediately following the publication of this book, we as individuals will communicate with images (both still and moving) as never before.

Just as educators since Gutenberg's time have taught their students to read (and create) letters and numbers, and charts and graphs have been printed and reproduced with paper and ink, today's educators must begin to foster in their students a new literacy that encompasses almost anything that can be digitally reproduced—images, sounds, video, and words.

Although at first this might sound extreme, in the past decade or so we have gone from a few computers transmitting text messages within a slow, secure, military-only network to high-speed, wireless file sharing of everything from your neighbor's baby photos to first-run Hollywood movies, all over the globe by way of the Internet. Whereas the primary source documents today's ten-year-olds are required to understand come from Gutenberg's tradition of printed words, the next generation of children will be learning to make sense of our digital movies and electronically composited photographs. The brave new world of digital publishing demands a brave new generation of educators to make sense of it all, side by side with their students.

A good place to start is with a cursory understanding of visual literacy. Photographs, charts, graphs, tables, and other forms of visual information are being digitized and posted online at an alarming rate, and advances in image search algorithms are making it more and more feasible to find information on the Net based primarily on its visual content. Websites such as the Library of Congress's American Memory Project are packaging important troves of archival photography in educator-friendly, searchable interfaces and posting them online for the public to use, free of charge.[5]

CCT's Image Detective website (http://www.edc.org/CCT/PMA/image_detective) is a great introduction to the science of decoding photographs for cultural and historical content. The site guides students and teachers step-by-step through the process of examining photographs through the eyes of an anthropologist (in this case Randy Bass, an American Studies scholar at Georgetown University) teaching them the basics of what to look for in an image.

The site addresses important concepts like being able to determine when and where a photograph was taken (without any textual evidence)—concepts that, while not necessarily difficult to understand, are at this point all but foreign to most of us.

Just like historians, students will pose questions to themselves as they look at the photos, like "Are these people rich, or poor, or in the middle?" . . . Next, students will scan the picture, looking for details that intrigue them. . . . Encourage students first to describe what they observe, without making any judgment. Then encourage them to speculate about what the detail might mean—to make intelligent guesses just like historians do.

Historians filter what they see through a vast amount of background knowledge—of the period, of similar documents, and of arguments about the past. Children's prior knowledge is far less—but they can use what they DO know very effectively. Ask students "What do you know about this?" "How is this different than what you'd expect?" Students can also read a little background about the picture and the time period by clicking the button. . . .

Just as historians talk with others to deepen their thinking about a document or a period, students looking at the COMPARE screen will compare their own interpretations to scholars', teachers', and other students'. Encourage them to note similarities and differences between their thinking and others', and use these insights as they tackle more interpretations.[6]

For while we have been schooled since an early age to read and write, most of us have never been taught anything about how to extract anything beyond cursory information from photographs and other visual imagery. Particularly when it comes to looking at photographs as primary sources of historical information, much can be gleamed from the details of a photograph with a little bit of training.

RICH MEDIA: THE MOVING IMAGE AND BEYOND

Understanding imagery is key to new media literacy because of the proliferation of imagery in the Internet age, but understanding the information contained in a still picture is just the beginning. The power of the networked personal computer has led to a veritable explosion in the average person's ability to produce and transmit digital media of all sorts, including motion pictures. As discussed before, the MiniDV camcorder and easy-to-use software like Apple's iMovie have brought professional-quality movie production to the home user. Thoughtful production of video in the classroom is not only a great way to teach your students about technology and storytelling, it can also be a hands-on lesson in media literacy.

Americans get much of their information from the television. Whether it's through learning about world events on the news, historical stories on PBS documentaries, or "life lessons" on fictional dramas and sitcoms (and, increasingly, "reality TV" shows), we assimilate what we watch on television into our worldviews.

Television producers wield an enormous amount of power and influence over our culture through the programming choices they make. News producers choose not only what stories do and don't make it onto a broadcast but also which details are included in an on-air segment and which get left on the cutting room floor. Editors can change the tenor of factual information in how they sequence footage, or what music or narration they lay underneath an image.

Much as editing is part and parcel of the writing process, so too is it paramount in the creation of television and multimedia at large. Guiding your students through the process of writing, filming, and editing a story will help them understand how the same process is used in the production of the media they consume in everyday life. Being able to recognize that editing decisions have been made in a TV news piece is the beginning of being able to investigate why those choices might have been made: Were all sides of a story given equal time? If not, why, and what was the effect of the bias? What's the difference between including all and some of an interview, and how does that impact the truth of the story you're telling? How can the emotional impact of a video clip be affected by the music or narration that accompanies it?

My generation was raised on MTV; I remember watching the channel for the first time shortly after it debuted on August 1, 1981. I had just turned eight and was visiting at my cousins' house—they had cable television and my family didn't. I sat down in front of MTV and literally didn't stop watching for the next eight hours. It wasn't just because I was an avid music fan, either (although that certainly was part of it).

The "programs" (music videos) were so short—just three or four minutes, as compared to the thirty-and sixty-minute TV shows I was used to—that it was all too easy to keep saying, "I'll just watch one more." One more became two became five became another several hours in front of the tube; the experience was not unlike the old Lay's potato chip commercials in which celebrities bet each other that they couldn't "eat just one." Between the novelty of the format and the easily digestible short-form programs, it proved impossible for me to watch just one music video.

To say that MTV and the hundreds of channels of glitzy, fast-edit cable television programming—to say nothing of the rise of video games and the personal computer—that followed in its wake gave birth to a generation of children stricken with attention deficit disorder would be beyond my scope of expertise. However, I think it is fair to say that today's viewer consumes television much differently than did the first generation of TV watchers in the '50s, '60s, and '70s.

Whether our attention spans are actually any shorter, with hundreds of channels of remote-controlled options literally at our fingertips, we have little incentive to be patient with story development on television. If one show doesn't catch our interest right away, surely something on the next channel will. And if not, it's easy to surf around the dial until we've come back to the beginning. With standard thirty- and sixty-minute programs interspersed with channels devoted exclusively to short-form programming (music videos, sports highlights, news/weather/financial information), there's almost always something new on at least one of the channels, so why waste your time on something boring?[7]

Understanding how we consume media and information is essential to beginning to redefine literacy in the 21st century. For better or for worse, children today are being reared on the quick sell. When I work with a class of fourth graders and find some of them growing frustrated with a computer that takes a few seconds to respond to their mouse clicks, I say, "Be patient." But why should these children have any cause for patience when so much of what we throw at them on television and on the radio, in video games and magazines, is engineered to be unwrapped, consumed, digested, and discarded in the blink of an eye?

Multimedia technology carries with it the power to shape all facets of communication—narrative, medium, transmission—in ways never before thought possible or even thought of at all. What producers of commercial television, video games, and websites are now doing is at the same time both cutting edge *and* merely the tip of the iceberg. While the majority of the dominant media outlets in our society are concerned only with using communication to market and sell products (and they've begun to master their trade quite effectively), artists, educators, and thinkers of all sorts are beginning to understand the power of multimedia to communicate rich information in multiple ways. We are also understanding how to make that communication a dialogue between all parties, and not just the one-way process of broadcast and consumption that big media relies on.

DL, VR, AND WEBQUESTS:
CUSTOMIZED MEDIA FOR LEARNING

One of the hardest and potentially most rewarding challenges facing the new media-literate teacher is leveraging the interactive nature of multimedia to create dynamic learning environments that adapt to the different needs of individual learners. The web, for instance, is popular and powerful because it literally has something for everyone. Short of turning students loose to browse whatever websites interest them, how can we harness the web's basic appeal to the individual in order to make learning more exciting, valuable, and fun for our students? Where is the balancing point between the one-size-fits-all-students lesson plans of days gone by and the free-for-all of unguided web surfing (or channel surfing, for that matter)?

Commercial publishing companies look for the answer in elaborate CD-ROM–based (and, more recently, web-based) software packages that adapt content to student performance. Typically, a title will contain a large database of content (for instance, algebra questions) and be programmed to start every user out with the same core set of instruction and exercises. As the student works his way through the content, his progress is measured and tracked, usually based on performance (e.g., how many questions were answered correctly and incorrectly). The program will then start to selectively choose further content based on performance: students who excel will be met with increasingly difficult or sophisticated material, while those who are struggling will be given extra practice or remedial content.

Educational software is available for almost every topic imaginable and at all grade levels, including adult learners. Delivery mediums range from basic onscreen text with a minimum of graphics to full-on multimedia environments in which students see and hear the material, while also interacting with the program via mouse, keyboard, or even spoken input.

Recent trends in commercial software publishing have centered on leveraging online content to enhance or extend CD-ROM programs. A math software package, for example, might come with a finite number of problem sets but include Internet access to "refills" that allow for extra practice. In this way, the manufacturer can take advantage of the large data capacity of the CD-ROM format to deliver the core software application, and then use the smaller bandwidth available online to deliver updates to the program.

Conversely, virtual universities and other Internet-based educational ventures are increasingly sending students CD-ROM content to supplement web-based courses. For instance, a course might be offered in real-time through a website offering text chat, text- and graphic-based documents, and perhaps some audio clips, all easily accessible via online downloads. Rich media supplements to the course—video files, most notably—would then be viewed from CD-ROM to avoid the bandwidth constraints of the Net. Clever programming can allow the website (or even the instructor via the website) to control media access from the CD, allowing for a seamless environment that combines an interactive, instructor-led, web-based virtual classroom with locally hosted rich media resources that most students can't access yet online.[8]

Many of the web-based distance learning programs available now use the Internet to eliminate the need for students to physically go to a classroom, but they still attempt to recreate our conventional learning environments online. Forward-thinking schools, universities, and commercial learning ventures are starting to experiment with designs for computer-aided learning that are built around the unique properties of the digital environment and not as attempts to re-create desks-and-books classrooms on the computer. The following are three different examples of interesting computer-based learning, employing technology at different levels of sophistication to serve different sets of learners.

Universal Design for Learning

The folks at the Center for Applied Special Technologies (CAST, http://www.cast.org/udl) in Wakefield, Massachusetts, have a simple mission that they approached armed with all the power of their passion and ingenuity: Make education accessible to all learners, regardless of their physical capabilities or impairments. CAST works toward this goal using the power of digital media to their advantage. As David Rose and Anne Meyer, co-executive directors of CAST, wrote in the March 2003 issue of *Cable in the Classroom*:

> Although digital media . . . represent information through text, sound, and images, the similarities to traditional media end there. By virtue of one essential feature—flexibility—digital media surpass traditional media in their ability to meet students' varied needs in a variety of instructional contexts. Digital media can save text, speech, and images reliably and precisely, and yet they offer tremendous flexibility in how and where those text, speech, and images can be redisplayed and adapted. Further, the inherent flexibility of digital media makes it possible to create curriculum with embedded learning supports that can, in turn, be individualized. This is very useful to teachers with diverse classrooms.[9]

While many people don't know about CAST, those who do often associate it with "special education." That is, they take the term *diverse classroom* to refer to an environment in which there are "normal" students and also those with "abnormal" learning disabilities brought about by physical and/or emotional handicaps.

The truth is, we all learn differently, and much as the PowerPoint, digital video, and other projects cited in Bank Street College's research (see chapter four) point to the power of digital media in supporting multiple learning styles, CAST's work seeks to leverage that same power to represent learning materials in different formats to suit different learners.

CAST's work in this area has led to what it calls a Universal Design for Learning (UDL). The principles of UDL are rooted in an architectural movement also called *universal design*, which was named by Ron Mace and centered on the idea of buildings designed from the outset to be accessible to everyone. The basic idea behind the movement was that physical structures that are "universally designed" from the ground up to include provisions for the physically disabled (elevators where there are stairs, access ramps at entrances, and so on) are more functional, cost efficient, and aesthetically pleasing than their traditionally designed counterparts that must later be retrofitted for accessibility. As Rose and Meyer wrote:

> Designing for the divergent needs of special populations increases usability for everyone. Because universal-designed buildings were superior to retrofitted

buildings functionally, aesthetically, and economically, schools of architecture began including courses on Universal Design and the movement spread to commercial products, landscape design, transportation, and many other fields. Universal Design does not imply "one size fits all" but rather acknowledges the need for alternatives to suit many different people's needs.[10]

Universal Design for Learning takes that same idea and applies it to the design of educational methods and materials. The creation (or retrofitting, in many cases) of universally accessible materials for learning need not be an expensive, labor-intensive venture, either. Using many of the same ubiquitous tools discussed in chapter four, CAST can take a standard text-based document and turn it into a prime example of flexible digital media for learning.

For example, a growing number of books and periodical articles that might be useful in the classroom are now available in electronic form, whether as web pages, .pdf (Adobe Acrobat) files, or proprietary e-books. An educator can use the basic principles of UDL (along with some knowledge of standard but seldom-used features of common computer software) to make electronic text more readily accessible to diverse learners.

Most web browsers, along with Acrobat Reader, Microsoft Word, and other software for viewing text, have one-click zooming functionality that lets users adjust the size of onscreen text. This is the electronic equivalent of printing a large-print edition of a book, just without the time, labor, and resource costs associated with print publishing. Score one for visually impaired learners.

Current versions of many of the same programs also have built-in text-to-speech capabilities that will read any selectable text aloud via synthesized voices "spoken" through the computer's speakers or headphones.[11] This can be a great help not only for giving the visually impaired access to print information (again, having a computer read an electronic file to you eliminates the need to republish the material as an audio book) but also for teaching reading and language skills.

Following along with text as it's being read aloud, for instance, can be a great way to learn and reinforce correct word pronunciations. Specialized software applications including CAST's own eReader program extend these features specifically for educational purposes, including features such as word-by-word highlighting synchronized to the computer's reading of a text and the use of high-quality, multilingual synthesized voices like AT&T's Digital Voices.

While copyright laws apply to educators using texts in their classrooms just like everyone else, there are provisions you should know about when it comes to reformatting copyrighted materials to provide greater accessibility to students. The Americans with Disabilities Act (ADA), Individuals with Disabilities Education Act (IDEA), Section 504 of the Rehabilitation Act, and the Chafee Amendment all pertain to educators (and other public service providers) and mandate accessibility to facilities and materials for the disabled.

The Chafee Amendment is particularly relevant here, as it "allows authorized entities to reproduce or distribute copies or phonorecords of previously published nondramatic literary works in specialized formats exclusively for use by blind or other persons with disabilities."[12] In other words, it's perfectly legal for you to create and/or distribute an audio CD or mp3 file of a copyrighted nondramatic work to students who are having trouble reading the text so they can listen to the work being read aloud. Yes, teachers are authorized entities. No, dramatic works of literature (plays, movie scripts, etc.) are not covered by Chafee. But, yes, Shakespeare is in the public domain, so go ahead and put *Hamlet* on your students' mp3 players so they can listen to it as they read.

The people of CAST are also hard at work on a number of proprietary UDL-based projects, including a very exciting multimedia textbook. The prototype version I saw provides multiple forms of access at every point of learning, including comprehension questions that can be read or listened to, myriad graphical icons for visual learners, and vocabulary glossaries supported by audio and video to best reach learners of all abilities and styles. Additionally, "Thinking Reader," based on CAST's UDL research, was (as of press time) just becoming available from Tom Snyder Productions/Scholastic (see www.tomsnyder.com)—a promising development for moving UDL into the mainstream.

Massachusetts Institute of Technology

The bullet-pointed table in the center of the MIT's OpenCourseWare home page (http://ocw.mit.edu) says it as well as anyone could. Posted to the web as a pilot in September 2002 and officially launched a year later, Massachusetts Institute of Technology's OpenCourseWare project is "about sharing knowledge." "This is not described as a learning initiative," explains

Table 5.1.

MIT OpenCourseWare is:	MIT OpenCourseWare is not:
• A publication of MIT course materials. • Free and open to the world.	• A degree- or certificate-granting program. • An MIT education.

Laura Koller, former director of production and publication, "but as a publication. We're publishing information, not creating an interactive website."

Koller was one of two people asked to project-manage OpenCourseWare when it was started in 2001 with "a lot of research and soul-searching on how to do something with online learning." Three years later, OpenCourseWare has a full staff of management, production, and faculty advisement teams, and is taking shape as MIT's attempt to spearhead a movement to share knowledge among universities around the world. "We turned over lots of ideas on commercial ventures and thought that the point shouldn't be about making money," Koller explained, "but rather that knowledge should be freely shared. This is in alignment with MIT's mission, and there is a strong institutional commitment to the project."

The basic idea is just that: Knowledge should be freely shared. MIT is not offering degrees, certifications, or classes of any kind via OpenCourseWare. Rather, the university is publishing materials for hundreds of their courses to the web for anyone, anywhere, to learn from. A timeline on the home page touts September 2003 as the official launch date with "over 500 courses" available, and September 2007 as the projected date when "virtually all" of MIT's courses will be published.

Right now, a few mouse clicks will get you a .pdf file entitled "Sensitization and Conditioning in Aplysia: Cellular Mechanisms" (from the Neural Basis of Learning and Memory, fall 2001, course 9.3, Department of Brain and Cognitive Sciences)[13] or the syllabus for the history department's spring 2002, course 21H.433, The Age of Reason: Europe in the 18th and 19th Centuries.[14] No, you're not getting a degree or any other sort of credentials from MIT, but you are getting knowledge, a free education in one sense of the word, from one of the world's most respected institutes of learning. Pretty amazing stuff!

Koller says that if the project is still going fifteen years from now, it will not be just at MIT. "This is a notion of a shared learning community at many places," she explained. "We would like to spread this idea but the trick is to make it sustainable (financially and otherwise) and be able to have other schools model it. That would be fulfilling. . . . The most fun part of the job is reading my e-mail every day—people from all over the world now having access to this is a great thing." She says that much of that e-mail is from people in low-tech, low-bandwidth areas of the world who have found the OpenCourseWare site and are grateful for it.

An article in *Wired* magazine coinciding with the official launch of Open-CourseWare in September 2003 cited the growing number of communities sprouting up all over the globe (both online and in person) to support group learning based on the MIT-provided content. As David Diamond wrote:

> One of the most popular offerings turned out to be Laboratory in Software Engineering, a.k.a. 6.170, a tough requirement for electrical engineering and computer science majors. Lam Vi Quoc, a fourth-year student at Vietnam's Natural Sciences University, relied on 6.170 lectures to supplement a software lab he was taking and to improve his coding skills. In Karachi, Pakistan, a group of 100 students and professionals met weekly to study 6.170. In Kansas City, five members of the Greater Kansas City Java Professionals Association gathered monthly to take the course. In Mauritius, a tiny island-nation in the Indian Ocean, Priya Durshini Thaunoo used 6.170 to prepare for a master's degree program at the University of Mauritius. Saman Zarandioon, an Iranian refugee living in Vienna, studied it to continue an education that was stalled by the Iranian government. And software developer Rahul Thadani in Birmingham, Alabama, took it to sharpen his skills.[15]

The majority of the course materials now online are text-based, supplemented by some graphics and .pdf files, and in some cases, video lectures. Not only does this format keep production costs down, it also makes the materials accessible to low-tech users. And, judging by the enthusiasm expressed by some of those users in their e-mails to Laura Koller and her colleagues, it may well be that OpenCourseWare is having the greatest impact on those very people who never dreamed they'd one day have access to MIT's knowledge base.

BronXplore—Teaching Matters

Teaching Matters (http://www.teachingmatters.org/xplore) is a non-profit organization located in New York City that works with teachers, students, and school administrators to bring the effective use of technology into schools throughout the five boroughs of New York City. Most of Teaching Matters's work is done in underperforming schools in some of the city's poorest neighborhoods, where resources, both financial and human, are at a premium. Community School District (CSD) 7, located in the Mott Haven section of the South Bronx, is no exception to this.

CSD 7 approached Teaching Matters about building a customized webquest just for them. They'd seen and used webquests in which students used the Net to learn about far-off places like the Australian Outback and the ancient ruins of Maya. What the folks in District 7 really wanted was a chance to use the web to learn about the history and culture of their home: The Bronx. Thus was born BronXplore.

Working with District 7's technology team, Teaching Matters built a web-based "backyard curriculum" all about The Bronx. At that time, I was part of the Teaching Matters team concentrating on this project. Since we were to be working with fourth graders that first year (2001–2002), we wrote a story about Manny and Sophie, twin brother and sister who had just arrived in The Bronx from San Diego. The twins needed to learn all about their new hometown; who better to show them around than their peers in District 7?

Following an online map of The Bronx, students completed interdisciplinary units based around particular places of interest in the borough. The introductory unit, set at District 7's offices, was all about geography and perspective; a visit to borough hall led to a unit about the workings of local government; The Bronx Zoo was home to a unit about animals, habitat, and other Earth science topics. Ample opportunities for core skills development were woven into the units (fourth graders in New York City schools face high-stakes math and English/language arts tests at the end of the year), and all of the lessons were aligned to city and state learning standards.

Being a web-based curriculum, BronXplore afforded many opportunities for technology integration in our partner schools. Lessons were designed around visits to free websites and hands-on work leveraging the ubiquitous tools mentioned in chapter four (word processing, e-mail, and so on). Ongoing e-mail exchanges between students and Teaching Matters's staff would be part of the curriculum and serve the dual purposes of teaching a technology skill and building reflections on learning into the coursework. All in all it was a clever, innovative, customized curriculum built on a tight budget.

Of course, what awaited us when we arrived at the different schools to work with the teachers was a little different from what we'd been planning for. One school I worked in had a seldom-used PC lab with twelve workstations and twenty chairs for the twenty-eight or so students in each class, and a totally unreliable Internet connection. The New York City Department of Education–installed security software locked the computers down so students couldn't save their work from session to session. Another school had a lab with more than thirty-five computers running on a well-maintained Windows NT network, and ongoing technology classes such that each student had an assigned computer and desk, a personal work folder on the network, and at least a year's worth of once-weekly technology classes under their belts.

The first school had AppleWorks installed on every computer, so we did all of our work using that software; the second school had MS Office installed on their computers and the fourth graders had been studying Microsoft Word and PowerPoint, so we used those tools. We knew how important it was to adapt to what students and circumstances threw our way, so adapt we did, as best we could.

Two years of teaching and managing the BronXplore program taught me a few things. First, kids like to use computers. Second, *high concept* is great when you're sitting around the planning table with a blank sheet of paper and a commission to create a dazzling, innovative technology project, but *simple* tends to work best when it comes to actually engaging students.

We built BronXplore around the narrative of new kids arriving in town from far off. That went over well. We also built a key component of the curriculum—reflection on learning—around the idea that students would role-play, pretending to be the twins reporting back to their fictitious Mom and Dad on what they'd learned about their new home. That didn't work so well; students were confused about who they were supposed to be and who they were writing to about what. One minute we were asking them to show their make-believe classmates around the town, the next minute we asked them to *be* the make-believe kids and write to their make-believe parents.

We also built certain lessons entirely around web-based resources. For instance, year one of the project culminated in a field trip to Yankee Stadium to watch the Bronx Bombers in action. Baseball can be educational, so we wrote a lesson about the history of the Yankees and the cultural and economic impact of the team on The Bronx. The lesson asked students to gather information and answer questions using the Yankees' website, as well as those of major league baseball and a few sports-related publications.

Unfortunately, sports websites are blocked from in-school access by NYCDOE Internet-filtering software. So we had our trip to a baseball game, but lost our chance to tie the team and stadium into the history of the neighborhood. Our revisions to the curriculum for year two included provisions for blocked websites or days when a school's Internet connection was down altogether. The future may be paperless, but the present sometimes demands hardcopy backups, just in case.

The point is that a backyard curriculum can be a great way to tie interdisciplinary skill development to a subject that students, parents, and educators can get excited about. No matter where you are, be it The Bronx, Bali, or Key Biscayne, your community is a veritable treasure trove of facts, legends, and local lore that span the academic spectrum from history to math and everything in between. Planning and writing a custom curriculum about your community takes hard work, but the results can be well worth the effort involved. Many progressive early childhood curriculums are based on studying neighborhoods and the people who live and work in them. Civic pride, knowledge of what makes your community work, and a sense of where you come from are valuable things for students of every age to learn.

The Internet can be a great resource in developing a backyard curriculum and sharing the results. Beyond high-profile websites about places like Yankee Stadium and The Bronx Zoo, community websites and newsgroups abound. There's a Yahoo! group for the block I live on in Brooklyn, and another for the neighborhood community association.16 There is likely a website or newsgroup for your town or neighborhood that could be a great resource in planning a backyard curriculum. Remember, not only can web resources be direct sources of information, they can also lead you to people who can become e-mail pen pals and guest speakers for your class.

BronXplore's final project was a student-made "Bronx the Beautiful" guide to the borough. Students used their newly developed technology skills to organize and design the information they gathered about The Bronx. The result was a pamphlet chock-full of history and information about the borough, including tips on what to do, what to see, and what to eat while in town. Ideally, a project like this could be printed out for the class to keep, and also published to the web as a community resource. That's the power of the Internet—no longer are we passive recipients of information only. Now everyone has the chance to share what they know with the world.

You may have been surprised to find out that MIT's OpenCourseWare initiative is primarily text-based. One of the world's leading technology universities should be using the most sophisticated stuff available when it comes to their distance learning programs, right? This is a good example of technology designed and employed to serve its audience. The goal of OpenCourseWare is to get materials out to as many people as possible, not to immerse them in state-of-the-art interactive environments. MIT has plenty of other programs that make use of the state of the art in digital technology; don't worry. But OpenCourseWare wouldn't be able to reach those grateful folks in the far-flung corners of the Earth if it wasn't so "low tech"—it wouldn't work with anything fancier.

When planning technology design for your students, you have to start with your goals as if you were planning any other educational activity. If the goal is to get information out via the Internet to as many people as possible all over the world (as in OpenCourseWare's case), a relatively low-tech, low-bandwidth solution like text-based web pages is the way to go.

In designing BronXplore, we knew we'd have some bandwidth and software hurdles to jump when working in underperforming New York City schools, but we also knew we had to engage and challenge fourth graders while showing them how meaningful working on a computer could be. We designed a colorful site with relatively low-bandwidth Flash animations and photographs of the places mentioned in the curriculum, the goal being to keep it simple yet fun and exciting.

CAST's goal in Universal Design for Learning is a little bit different. UDL is a philosophy to be learned and applied to any and all educational settings. Whether you're working on a website, CD-ROM, or with a chalkboard and copy machine, you can design activities and materials to support all learners, regardless of physical ability or learning style. Of course, one of the core aims of UDL is to leverage the flexibility of digital media toward this aim, and as the medium matures and as the power, speed, and accessibility of the Internet and personal computers continues to grow, educators will be able to do more and more with sound, video, and interactive media to help their students learn.

Whatever your goals in using digital media to help your students learn, it is important to recognize the sea change that has begun when it comes to how we communicate with one another with the aid of technology. Digital media is changing what is possible when it comes to creating, capturing, and communicating information, and the Internet makes it easier with each passing day to transmit that information to your friends, neighbors, and those around the globe.

Being able to support your students as they learn to "speak digital" isn't about "keeping up with the Joneses" or impressing parents on Open House night; it's about understanding that something at the heart of our society is changing, and taking advantage of the enormous opportunity that is part and parcel of that change.

Digital media already carries with it a great promise. For educators, a large part of that promise lies in the potential to support individual learners with materials and programs better tailored to their needs. Computers will never take the place of good teachers, and interactive media is no substitute for conversation and discussion among students, teachers, and families. But if a printed text can be reproduced in large type, translated to Spanish, augmented with a glossary and images or video to help with word definitions, and read aloud while a struggling reader follows along onscreen, our good teachers will have another tool to help them help their students. And if digital media and the Internet make the production and dissemination of computerized materials cheap and easy, more teachers and students will be able to use them.

The better equipped you and your students are to read and write multimedia, so to speak, the more able you will become to contribute to your community. And in this Internet-connected digital age, the whole world truly is your community.

NOTES

1. Cornelia Brunner and William Talley, *The New Media Literacy Handbook* (New York: Anchor Books, 1999), 18.

2. A new generation of digital cable, driven by computer-like "set-top boxes," promises to change the way we interact with television, combining traditional viewing with Internet-like functionality. Although services such as WebTV have

been on the U.S. market for several years now, they haven't caught on or developed as extensively as European interactive television offerings. Such programming, controlled by a souped-up remote control device, combines traditional television fare with program-specific special features, such as the ability to call up background information or statistics during news and sports programming, or automated ordering and payment applications within shopping shows. As was the case with videotape and cell phone standards before, the splintered U.S. market is slowing down the widespread adoption and implementation of interactive television.

3. Brunner and Talley, *The New Media Literacy Handbook*, 38.

4. Taken from 2002–2003 New York City Department of Education Scope and Sequence for Learning, Social Studies Grade 4, as appears at http://www.nycenet.edu/dis/scopesequence/socialstudies46.html

5. http://memory.loc.gov/ammem/amhome.html

6. http://www.edc.org/CCT/PMA/image_detective/method.html

7. An in-depth, academic analysis of the style, structure, and cultural impact of music television can be found in Andrew Goodwin's *Dancing in the Distraction Factory* (see the following suggested reading list).

8. As bandwidth becomes more widespread, this will be less and less of an issue. The growth of DSL, cable, and fiber-optic Internet connections allows software makers to deliver more and more software packages and large updates to programs via the Internet without the need for conventional delivery on CD-ROM and other "physical" media. Constraints associated with the need for physical delivery of data will continue to lessen as time goes on.

9. David Rose and Anne Meyer, "Digital Learning," *Cable in the Classroom* (March 2003), 1–4.

10. David Rose and Anne Meyer, "Universal Design for Learning," *JSET eJournal* 15, no. 1 (winter 2000), Associate Editor column. Available online at http://jset.unlv.edu/15.1/asseds/rose.html

11. Apple Macintosh operating systems have a built-in text-to-speech engine; OS X features systemwide text-to-speech support for most applications. Different flavors of the Microsoft Windows operating system offer varying levels of text-to-speech capabilities.

12. http://www.loc.gov/nls/reference/factsheets/copyright.html

13. http://ocw.mit.edu/NR/rdonlyres/33145F32-652A-4A6F-8965-4D0B4E813209/0/903lec4/pdf

14. http://ocw.mit.edu/OcwWeb/History/21H-433The-Age-of-Reason-Europe-in-the-18th-and-19th-CenturiesSpring2002/Syllabus/index.htm

15. David Diamond, "MIT Everywhere," *Wired* (September 2003), 135–36.

16. Yahoo! groups (http://groups.yahoo.com) are listservs sponsored and hosted by Yahoo! There are a number of companies that provide listserv hosting services for free or a small fee, or you can run your own listserv if you have access to a web server. Yahoo! groups are popular right now because they are free to use (though you have to deal with the occasional advertisement) and many people are familiar with the name.

SUGGESTED READING

Don DeLillo, *Underworld* (New York: Scribner, 1997).

――, *White Noise* (New York: Viking Press, 1985).

William Gibson, *Neuromancer* (New York: Ace Books, 1994), reprint edition.

――, *Pattern Recognition* (New York: Putnam, 2003).

Andrew Goodwin, *Dancing in the Distraction Factory: Music Television and Popular Culture* (Minneapolis: University of Minnesota Press, 1992).

David Pogue

David Pogue's books, newspaper columns, and other writings on technology are a treasure trove of insights, tips, and humor on technology in today's world. Educators tend to enjoy Pogue's work as he's very adept at translating tech-speak into language that the not-so-tech literate can understand. Pogue is also one of the leading authors of how-to books for all things related to the Apple Macintosh, though he has written equally well about other computer systems. Of particular relevance to this chapter are these books on Apple's digital photography and video software: *iMovie 3 and iDVD: The Missing Manual* (Sebastapol, Calif.: O'Reilly and Associates, 2003) and *iPhoto 2: The Missing Manual* (Sebastapol, Calif.: O'Reilly and Associates, 2003).

Neal Stephenson, *Snow Crash* (New York: Bantam, 1992).

SUGGESTED WEB LINKS

Media Literacy

The American Memory Project, http://memory.loc.gov/

CCT Image Detective, http://www.edc.org/CCT/PMA/image_detective/index.html

CCT Media Literacy, http://www2.edc.org/CCT/topic.asp?numTopicId=11

Special Education and Educational Technology Resources

Journal of Special Education Technology—JSET eJournal, http://jset.unlv.edu/

Copyright Laws and Fair Usage of Materials in Education

http://www.mediafestival.org/copyright.pdf

Pogue's Pages, website of NY Times columnist and author David Pogue

http://www.davidpogue.com/

Learning Digital Photography

Arthur Bleich's Digital Photography Corner, http://www.dpcorner.com/
Yahoo! Groups Digital Photography Group, http://dir.yahoo.com/Arts/
Visual_Arts/Photography/Digital/

Learning Digital Video

Apple iMovie and Digital Video Source List, http://www.leoniaschools
.org/dv/SourceList.html
Beginner's Guide to Digital Video Production, http://www.dvmoviemaking.com/
Digital Video for Teachers, http://dvforteachers.manilasites.com/
Yahoo! Groups Digital Video Group, http://groups.yahoo.com/group/Digital_
Video/

Chapter Six

In Conclusion: What to Do
When the Lights Go Out

August 14, 2003: I am sitting at the table in the living room of my new apartment in Brooklyn, New York, when I notice that the lamp has gone dim. The late afternoon sun still illuminates the room, so it may have been several minutes since the lights went out. Did the bulb blow? The top of my laptop's screen shows that I'm now running on battery power, and a quick look around the apartment shows that the digital clocks have gone dark, as well. The power is out.

Twenty minutes and two trips downstairs to consult with my neighbor later, I find out that the power is, in fact, out in the whole building. Actually, the power's gone out all over New York City, upstate to Canada, and as far west as Michigan and Ohio. In what TV news reporters were already calling "the Great Blackout of '03," a glitch in the system took out the entire grid that brings electricity to much of the northeast United States and parts of southeast Canada as well.

Some fifty million customers across 1,500 miles would go without electricity for anywhere from a few minutes to more than a day. In my case, the lights would stay out for about seventeen hours, from just after 4 P.M. on Thursday until 9 A.M. Friday. It was hot and it was dark, but the food in the fridge stayed cold, the water kept running, and my girlfriend made it back from Manhattan just fine, though she had to walk over the Brooklyn Bridge as it swayed under the weight of literally thousands of pedestrians.

I didn't finish my manuscript that night, as my computer's battery ran out faster than I could work. But we managed to get out of the city and on to our vacation the next day, and the fact that you're reading this is a testament to backup plans. I contacted my editor, she contacted the publisher, and we went on to Plan B.

Things don't always work as planned, and it's important to be able to think on your feet whether you're writing a book, teaching a class, or stranded in Manhattan when the lights go out. We can't be prepared for everything, but having a backup plan for when things go wrong is an invaluable resource as a teacher, especially if you're using computers and the Internet in your lessons. Network connections fail, hardware breaks, software locks up, and sometimes the lights go out altogether. These things happen, and sometimes they happen when you're in charge of thirty eleven-year-olds and are just about to begin a lesson that absolutely needs all systems running in order to work.

Even the best lesson plan in your curriculum binder won't do you any good if you don't have the resources you need to make it happen. So what to do when you're the technology teacher and all the power shuts off? Here are a couple of things to keep in mind.

First, always have some backup lessons that don't depend on technology. During my first year teaching BronXplore, the district office scheduled an end-of-year trip to a Yankees game to celebrate the project, and we were asked to develop a special unit on the history of the Bronx Bombers to lend some educational value to the trip. I researched the history of the team and the impact that the building of Yankee Stadium had on the economic and social development of The Bronx, and designed two short lessons that made use of Yankee-related websites. I had one visit left to my school before the Yankee field trip, and my plan was to take students through the first lesson in class and leave the second lesson for them to do with their teachers before the game.

Well, when I got to school everything fell apart in an instant: The Department of Education Internet-filtering software wouldn't let me into any of the websites used in the lessons. The Yankees are a baseball team, of course, and all of the websites were on sports-related sites (even though they contained a lot of great information about the history and development of The Bronx). Sports sites are one of the categories of forbidden places on the web in the eyes of the NYCDOE, and sure enough, all of my sites were on the restricted list. Twenty minutes before six classes of fourth graders are supposed to learn about Yankee Stadium, I'm reduced to saying, "The dog ate my websites."

What I should have done is tried ahead of time to access the websites from a school computer to make sure they would be available in class; I wrote the lesson at home using my unfiltered Internet connection. Then I would have known that the sites were blocked, and I could have either found different resources to use, brought hard copies of the information with me, or better yet, downloaded the sites to disk and loaded them onto the school machines for offline browsing.[1]

This way, even if the students couldn't get to the live site themselves, I would have had some way of giving them the materials for the lesson. Even if the activity had to be quickly restructured as, say, less individual student exploration than group discussion of the material, at least I could have salvaged the lesson. Instead, I was stuck.

This is not to say that you need to print backup copies of every web page you ever plan to use in class. But if something essential to your lesson is only available in electronic form, have a plan for what to do in case that resource is unavailable in your classroom.

Check to see that websites are accessible before class begins; this extends beyond Internet filtering to issues of software requirements, as sites that make use of animation, audio, video, or interactive media may not run on all computers (especially the older ones). Make sure that nonelectronic versions of the materials are available for substitution, and have backup lessons in case you need to postpone your plans until resources become available again. When the Internet connection in your classroom goes down, sometimes it's for five minutes and sometimes it's all day. Unless you're in charge of your school's network, it's hard to know how long you'll be down, so have something else ready to do with your class's time.

Second, remember that technology need not be harnessed to a computer. Yes, if we're teaching technology we should be concerned with helping our students learn practical, tangible computer skills. But technology still extends beyond the screen. Using a digital camera to document your class's work on nontechnology projects is learning about technology. Talking about the impact of mass media on us as a society and individuals is learning about technology. Using a yellow highlighter, to paraphrase Marvin Cohen, is also learning about technology.

The point is, for all of the emphasis placed on teaching computer skills, taking a step back to discuss what all of this technology means to us is an important element of the process that's all too often overlooked.

Just because we *can* do something does not mean that we *should* do it, and this is certainly true when it comes to computers. So many new products, programs, and philosophies surrounding the use of computers are hatched each day that it's worth spending some time considering what to teach and discuss and what to leave out.

Yes, it's important to learn to type, to learn to e-mail, and to learn to surf the web. Failing to understand that every day more people are relying on the Internet as a source of communication and information would be failing to understand what is happening to our society as a whole. But no, just because people are building websites does not mean that you or your students must become expert graphic designers and programmers.

It's important to know what's out there to explore, and it's just as important to think critically about what you need to know, want to know, and can just as well leave others to know. Teaching your students the ins and outs of Adobe Photoshop just because someone at the school down the road is doing it is not a pedagogically sound use of time. Teaching them Photoshop because they want or need to learn in order to produce the student newspaper, which is central to the journalism program, is another story.

Finally, at the risk of ending on a cliché, don't forget to teach your students to talk and listen to one another, to take deep breaths, and to go outside and look at the stars on clear nights. Mankind has produced some pretty amazing things and will continue to do so for as long as we're around. But no matter how sophisticated a virtual landscape we might build on our computers and across our networks, we still inhabit a world full of natural wonder that's well worth our time, attention, and consideration.

The most wondrous thing we have in the world is each other. Is it really so surprising that most of the time people spend online is spent in chat rooms, on bulletin boards, and perusing personal ads? It shouldn't be. Education is about learning about ourselves and one another, and it's also about trying to understand just what makes us all so unique and yet so much the same. Technology is a tool we can use to that end. Just remember, for all of those computers, digital cameras, and cell phones sending and receiving data across all of those fiber-optic cables and wireless networks, there are human beings at both ends of the line trying to make sense of it all.

Really, what we're doing is trying to make sense of one another.

NOTE

1. Of course, using a blocked website in school is subject to school and district regulations and approval from appropriate school officials. Additionally, making print or electronic copies of copyrighted material is subject to local and federal law. While many publishers don't mind the reproduction of their materials for educational use, you should obtain prior permission where necessary. Some websites are also programmed to block printing or downloading of content.

Glossary

alias—in a computer operating system, a shortcut

ARPANET—The precursor to the Internet, ARPANET was a large wide-area network created by the United States Defense Advanced Research Project Agency (ARPA) in 1969.

ASCII—The American Standard Code for Information Interchange. ASCII is the common code for microcomputer equipment. The standard ASCII character set consists of 128 decimal numbers ranging from zero through 127 assigned to letters, numbers, punctuation marks, and the most common special characters. The Extended ASCII Character Set also consists of 128 decimal numbers and ranges from 128 through 255 representing additional special, mathematical, graphic, and foreign characters.

bandwidth—Often used to refer to how much information can flow between computers connected to the Internet, bandwidth is the amount of data that can be transmitted in a fixed amount of time. For digital devices, the bandwidth is usually expressed in bits per second (bps) or bytes per second. For analog devices, the bandwidth is expressed in cycles per second, or Hertz (Hz).

BBS—Bulletin Board System

binary code—Binary refers to a numerical system that only uses two digits: 0 and 1. Computers use the binary system; binary code refers to coded instructions comprised solely of 0s and 1s, which often indicate whether a particular switch is Off (0) or On (1).

broadband—"Broadband transmission" is a type of data transmission in which a single medium can carry many channels at once. For our purposes, "broadband" refers to high-speed Internet connections such as T1 lines, DSL, and cable modems, as opposed to slower "dial up" (modem-based) connections.

CD—Compact Disc, a type of optical disc used for storing music. Can be played back on a computer or in a consumer audio CD player.

CD-R / CD-RW—Compact Disc Recordable / ReWriteable, a type of blank CD that can be "burned," or encoded with data using consumer equipment. CD-Rs can only be recorded to once, while CD-RWs are re-recordable.

CD-ROM—Compact Disc Read-Only Memory, a type of optical disc that can be encoded with up to 1 gigabyte of data. Most modern computers have CD-ROM drives capable of reading both audio CDs and data CD-ROMs.

chat room—An Internet space in which multiple users may "chat" with one another via a text-based system. As broadband connections become widespread, "audio chat" and "video chat" are supplanting text-only chat rooms.

convergence—A generic term referring to combining some of the features and attributes of two existing technologies. Within the Internet community, it is often meant to describe the forthcoming infusion of telecommunications-aided interactivity into everyday technologies, e.g., "Interactive Television," "Interactive Textbooks."

CRT—Cathode Ray Tube, a common type of desktop computer monitor. These are the large "old style" monitors, not to be confused with "flat screen" or panel displays, which are often LCD-based.

cyberspace—A generic term describing the nonphysical or virtual space created by networked computer systems. Most everyday users are referring to the Internet (including the web and e-mail and chat systems) when they use the term cyberspace.

dot-com—A slang term describing an Internet-based business. Takes its name from the ".com" (commerce) domain assigned to commercial websites, e.g., Amazon.com, ebay.com. "Dot coms" usually refer to the many start-up web companies borne out of the Internet boom of the late 1990s.

DSL—Digital Subscriber Line. A broadband Internet connection delivered to homes and business over a standard phone line.

DVD—Digital Video Disc (or Digital Versatile Disc), a type of optical disc used for storing audiovisual content. Similar form factor to a CD, but holds up to 4.7 gigabytes of data. Commonly used for the commercial distribution of feature-length movies.

DVD-A—An audio form of the DVD medium, meant to hold more data and therefore provide richer sound over more audio channels than a CD.

DVD-ROM / R / RW—Similar to the CD-ROM / R / RW formats, DVDs can be used to encode and retrieve data on personal computers. Many personal computers now come equipped with DVD-ROM drives, which can be used to retrieve data and play DVD movies. DVD-R/RW discs can be burned with data using consumer-grade blank media.

DVR—Digital Video Recorder, also called PVR (Personal Video Recorder). A hard-drive based system for recording and playing back television, similar to tape-based VCRs. PVRs allow for advanced viewing options such as pausing and rewinding "live" broadcasts, digital freeze-frame and zoom, and Internet-based services such as viewers' guides and remote programming. TiVo and Replay TV are two popular brands of PVRs.

e-mail—electronic mail

guerilla marketing—Etymological offspring of "guerilla warfare," refers to unconventional advertising techniques that leverage creativity, intelligence, and low-cost broadcast methods to compete with large, well-funded competitors' advertising. The spread of e-mail and the web has borne a new generation of guerilla marketers who can take advantage of automated address harvesting and e-mail systems to spread their messages to many recipients at a very low monetary cost. Abuse of guerilla marketing tactics over e-mail can lead to "spam."

home page—The first page you see when surfing a particular website. Usually hosted at "/index.html," this is the page that any domain on the web points to. For example, when you surf to www.threebase.com, you get the Threebase home page, which is really www.threebase.com/index.html.

HTML—HyperText Markup Language, the common language of the World Wide Web

hyperlinks—A variant of HyperText, hyperlinks are areas on the web that are programmed to link, or lead to, other websites. Hyperlinks can be text, graphics, or other medium, though generally the term is used to refer to text. Also known as "hotlinks."

icons—small images used to represent an object or program in a computer system

IM—Instant Message

Information Superhighway—Generic term used to describe all of cyberspace as relates to giving people access to information. For example, "SuperData home DSL is your on-ramp to the Information Superhighway!" Thrown around by marketers and politicians in the late 1990s, the term has fallen out of favor.

I/O solutions—Input/Output solutions; refers to a means of getting data in and out of a computer. Often used to refer to hardware-based systems for digitizing audiovisual data from an analog source; that is, converting audio or videotape to a file format suitable for editing on a personal computer.

Listservs—"An automatic mailing list server developed by Eric Thomas for BITNET in 1986. When e-mail is addressed to a LISTSERV mailing list, it is automatically broadcast to everyone on the list. The result is similar to a newsgroup or forum, except that the messages are transmitted as e-mail and are therefore available only to individuals on the list. LISTSERV is currently a commercial product marketed by L-Soft International. Although LISTSERV refers to a specific mailing list server, the term is sometimes used incorrectly to refer to any mailing list server." (from webopedia.com)

LOGO—A computer programming language developed at MIT to be used to teach children mathematical concepts. Commonly known as "the turtle program" as it first featured an on-screen turtle that users would program to do various tasks such as moving and drawing.

menu bars—Toolbars within computer applications—usually pull-down menus located at top of the screen—that give access to common commands. The "File" menu is perhaps the most common menu bar.

meta-engine—In this context, a search engine that operates by utilizing other search engines to run multiple instances of the same search. The meta-engine then culls the results from the other engines and presents them to the user in its own formatting. Copernic is an example of a meta-search engine that leverages multiple search engines in an attempt to provide the most comprehensive search results possible.

modem—Short for modulator-demodulator, a software or hardware device that allows computers to connect and transmit data over phone or cable lines. Modem speeds are "baud-rate" (for slower modems) and bits per second for faster modems such as "56K" modems, which can transmit at up to 57,600 bps. Telephone modem-based "dial up" Internet connections are very popular although they are being surpassed now by faster cable modem and DSL connections.

Netizen—a citizen of the Net

PC—Personal Computer, sometimes used to refer specifically to Windows-based computers, e.g., "Do you use a PC or a Mac?"

PDA—Personal Digital Assistant, often used to refer to a Palm Pilot, though the term generically refers to any handheld, portable digital device that combines scheduling and organizational tools, sometimes alongside Internet/networking capacities and entertainment features such as games, digital cameras, and digital audio/video playback.

PIM—Personal Information Manager, a genre of software encompassing schedulers, organizers, address books, and other tools for managing "personal" information. Virtually all new PDAs and PCs, and many new cell phones, come with some sort of PIM software.

PVR—Personal Video Recorder. *See also* DVR.

QWERTY—Refers to the name given to the standard arrangement of keys on the English keyboard, designed in 1868 by Christopher Sholes, the inventor of the typewriter. Pronounced "kwer-tee."

search engine—A program that searches for keywords within a document, the term is used here to refer mainly to web-based resources that allow users to search the Internet for specific information.

UNIX—a popular computer operating system developed at Bell Labs in the 1970s

URL—Uniform Resource Locator; commonly known as the "address" of a website, URLs can actually be used to point to web pages and Internet-hosted resources. A URL beginning with http:// will point to a web page viewable via the http protocol, where as one beginning with ftp:// will point to a "fetchable" document accessible by the FTP protocol.

USENET—Global BBS that can be accessed via the Internet. USENET encompasses thousands of newsgroups in which virtually every topic imaginable is discussed by people around the world.

user interface—The system by which the user of a computer application navigates documents and program functionality. User interfaces can be text-based or graphical (GUI). The quality of an application's user interface is often referred to as its "usability."

VAX—Short for *Virtual Address eXtension*, a computer system introduced by Digital in 1977. VAX terminals were popular in schools, libraries, and other public and business settings through the 1980s and early '90s.

VCR—Video Cassette Recorder

VHS—A popular type of re-recordable videocassette tape used for consumer recording of television and movies. VHS beat out Beta to gain the lion's share of the consumer market, and virtually all movie rental stores now stock VHS tapes. DVD is fast outpacing VHS as the medium of choice for distribution of commercial video, and consumer-grade DVD recorders are beginning to infiltrate the market as well.

WWW—World Wide Web

webrings—A community of websites defined by a common subject matter and linked together by their webmasters. Often denoted by a "Part of the _____ Webring" slogan accompanied by relevant hyperlinks at the bottom of a homepage.

websites—Collections of web pages on the World Wide Web that fall under the care of one webmaster. More colloquially, the term is used interchangeably with "web pages," however, a web page technically refers to one page only whereas a website is *all* of the pages encompassed by, for example, www.scarecroweducation.com.

WYSIWYG—What You See Is What You Get, an acronym referring to a genre of computer applications that let you design a document (for print, web publication, etc.) based on visual layout as opposed to programming structures.

Index

About the Author

Noah Kravitz is an educator, writer, and musician who has worked extensively using technology to help children and adults learn. He currently works as an educational technology specialist in the New York City public school system and as the reviews editor for PowerBookCentral.com. Noah lives in Brooklyn, New York, and makes his virtual home on the web at www.threebase.com.